"*How We Love Matters* is an invitation for God's beloved community to sit at the table and enter into each other's narratives for the sake of true unity. For years I've had a front-row seat to witness one of America's best communicators. But Albert is not just a talking head. He has poured out his life to be a vessel of ethnic unity. This book is a timely and necessary offering, guaranteed to inspire you."

—Dr. Bryan Loritts, author of *Insider Outsider*

"Albert Tate's character and excellent communication skills consistently shine God's light in *How We Love Matters*. This book is for everyone who wants to see God's Kingdom now and forever expressed by every tribe, tongue, and nation gathering diversely, equitably, and inclusively at the table of Jesus. In other words, *How We Love Matters* is a MUST-read for every follower of Jesus!"

—Greg Nettle, president of Stadia Church Planting

"Albert Tate does what very few authors have the capacity to do. Pastor Tate is uniquely gifted by God to surgically cut to the heart with convicting truth but to do so with thoughtfulness, humor, and grace. This text emerges from the sensitivity and heart of a pastor of a multiethnic church as he offers uncompromised truths and inspirational stories that offer a hopeful narrative of what could be in the church."

—Soong-Chan Rah

"What Albert Tate gives us here is priceless. It's his life and heart. It's his story and family. It's his pain and ache. It's his anger and hope. It's his conviction and courage. It's his Gospel: why love matters."

—Dr. Mark Labberton, president of Fuller Theological Seminary

"Rooted in biblical truth, combining searing memoir and incisive cultural commentary, *How We Love Matters* is a powerful book for today. Albert Tate writes with prophetic urgency. He does not flinch from addressing the church's sin and complicity in the area of racism and systemic injustice. But he doesn't end there; Albert calls us away from a shallow response, reminding us of the power of the gospel to bring true redemption and reconciliation. May God's people hear these vital words, take them to heart, and then—live the life."

—Jo Saxton, leadership coach and author of *Ready to Rise*

"Pastor Albert Tate has really created an incredible framework for anyone who reads this work. *How We Love Matters* will go down in history as a literary catalyst for racial reconciliation, not only in the church but in every area where people's lives intersect. If you are really serious about understanding how to love your brother or sister who may not look like you, this resource is all you need."   —Erica and Warryn Campbell

"*How We Love Matters* is the book we need for the soul of the church. Albert reveals how racism continues to exist in the church today, but also provides tangible steps to reconciliation. As a father and pastor, my goal is to provide a life and a church for my children where they can grow in their love for Jesus and live a godly life. My prayer is that this book would inspire the necessary change in us, so that we can continue to build a world that reflects Jesus and His values for the next generation."   —Chad Veach, pastor of Zoe Church

"Albert has done a great thing for us by writing *How We Love Matters*. As the founding and lead pastor of a beautiful, vibrant, multiethnic church, Albert is writing what he is living. His well-written words are backed up by a well-lived life of gospel-shaped ethnic reconciliation. As you read, you will laugh and cry simultaneously; you will be relentlessly encouraged and challenged. But above all, you will get a glimpse of one who is love, King Jesus, and how He has surprised the world by reconciling enemies and making them friends."

—Dr. Derwin L. Gray, co-founder and lead pastor of
Transformation Church and author of *How to Heal the
Racial Divide: What the Bible Says, and the First
Christians Knew, about Racial Reconciliation*

"Some leaders teach what Scripture has to say about racial justice. Others wisely live it out with their family, church, and community. Albert does both—with courage, compassion, and conviction. In the many years I've known Albert, he has instructed and inspired me to wholeheartedly pursue the gospel's command to disciple out racism. I know this book will do the same for you."

—Kara Powell, PhD, chief of leadership formation at
Fuller Seminary, executive director of the Fuller Youth Institute,
and co-author of 3 *Big Questions that Change Every Teenager*

"This will easily be one of the most important books you read this year. In a world that seemingly grows more fractured, polarized, and divided by the second, we need Pastor Albert Tate's prophetic fire that calls us in, calls us out, and calls us up to see what must be done for racial reconciliation to become a reality."

—Steve Carter, pastor and author of
The Thing Beneath the Thing

"We all need to learn how to love better, especially now. That's why I'm so excited about this book. Albert Tate is an amazing man, mentor, and friend whose ministry has had a profound impact on me both up close and from afar. I've seen him on pulpits, prisons, and patios, teaching and preaching to anyone who would listen. I've seen their lives changed through his words. I've seen mine changed as well. His words have now found paper and the stories have come to life. Join Albert on this journey of navigating through difficult but necessary conversations on race, justice, and loving people well. You'll be glad you came."
—Sam Acho

"Many preachers/prophets and proclaimers of philosophical, intellectual, and theological truth stand in the pulpit, the podium, and the platform as reporters, researchers, and recorders of reflective products of their efforts. Some as expositors of historical texts, some as echoes of contemporary culture—echoes. Every now and then God releases a voice, not an echo of the loudest exclamations, but a voice of experiential truth. Such is the case with Albert Tate. His is a fresh voice for such a time as this. In this work his voice effectively balances exposition and experience, achieving the goal of connecting timeless gospel principles of justice and unity in the context of the contemporary life of followers of Christ. Welcome to a journey into the divine possibility of unity, oneness, and practical spirituality. You will see yourself as a recipient in each creatively addressed chapter to a 'dear' reader. Prepare to be encouraged, inspired, challenged, and changed."
—Bishop Kenneth Ulmer

"Albert Tate never stops teaching me. His insights and wisdom are truly gifts to my soul. I highly recommend *How We Love Matters* as a deep, wise, honest, and transformational read! This content is the remedy for our weary souls."
—Danielle Strickland

"*How We Love Matters* is an honest, challenging, and heartfelt call to action for all of us. Albert speaks with an authenticity and expertise that is engaging and captivating. His lifelong work in racial reconciliation lends credibility to the conversation of this book. I have tremendous respect and admiration for Albert and am immensely thankful for God's hand on his life to call us to more fully reflect Christ in how we love one another." —Bryan Carter

"In *How We Love Matters*, my best friend of thirty-five years, Albert Tate, has responded courageously to the demands our forebears at Sweet Home Church in Pearl, Mississippi, left us—lift every voice and sing. There are voices missing at the table of gospel-centered racial reconciliation. It's a voice our nation has to hear as we labor to put the pieces of oneness together for Christ's sake. Having shepherded in multiethnic churches for two decades, Albert knows better than anyone how easy it is to speak of reconciliation and how arduous the path is to make it happen. He's walked across the aisles. He's practiced what he's preaching. He's got a ministry chockfull of credibility through which to stretch us as much as he does. In some of the stories you'll read in this narrative, I was right there. Those unforgettable experiences shaped us, stretched us, in many ways scared us, but ultimately beckoned us to fight for a better world for our kids. And a better world for yours as well. The middle wall of partition has been removed. Let's keep it that way. Read this book!" —Ricky Jenkins, senior pastor of Southwest Church

"A daring conversation about the big problem of racism...with the masterful solution! *How We Love Matters* is here at the perfect time. Albert Tate daringly offers his perspective while brilliantly challenging our thinking. I'm confident that each reader of this masterpiece will be enlightened and will experience the growth needed for the times we live in." —Nissan Stewart

"In an era filled with people scrambling to achieve the appearance and culture of diversity, there are some who stand out as more authentic and relevant than others. Many voices are crying out for racial reconciliation but have forgotten that reconciliation requires more than a message. It requires a commitment to creating a table where all of our brothers and sisters can be truly heard and valued. Albert Tate is a pivotal and critical voice in this hour and his message of *How We Love Matters* is brilliant and convicting. If we fail the love test, we will potentially miss an opportunity to begin to move toward significant changes in the world as it relates to racial reconciliation. I have experienced the mission, the ministry, and the man Albert Tate. Though he masterfully communicates his heart for deep reconciliation with words, he lives it out every day even more authentically. This book should be on the shelves of every pastor, leader, creative, and entrepreneur who wants to create a culture of value and honor because how we love truly matters."

—Aaron W Lindsey, president and CEO of Prime Virtual
Solutions and six-time Grammy-winning producer/songwriter

"Love isn't a word we hear much in the midst of the current milieu we are in today. We see bickering and challenge, but rarely is the word love brought to us as a foundation for our interaction. Albert Tate is the perfect one to talk about this, because his ministry has been a model of what it looks like to fight for love. I'm hoping that this work will be yet another tool that leads to us fighting from the unity we have in Jesus versus trying to create unity by our own means."

—Eric Mason

"Over the past few years, God has used the preaching gift of Albert Tate to bless the body of Christ generally, and our Pinelake Church family specifically. Now, in *How We Love Matters*, my friend and brother uses his unique combination of hard-hitting truth, quick wit, and keen biblical insight to call the body of Christ to live out the reconciliation purchased by the blood of Jesus. This book is timely, inspiring, challenging, and desperately needed to restore hope and ignite a passion to see reconciliation become reality in the FAMILY of faith."

—Chip Henderson, senior pastor of Pinelake Church

"My brother and friend Albert Tate has brilliantly written a series of timely and important letters that make up *How We Love Matters: The Practice of Relentless Racial Reconciliation*. In an era where many want to ignore the sin of racism, Tate masterfully weaves together scriptural inspiration and culturally relevant stories to challenge us to love like Jesus. *How We Love Matters* is a must-read book for everyone who believes that love of Jesus is the cure for the ill of racism."

—Dave Ferguson, lead pastor of Community Christian Church and author of *B.L.E.S.S.: 5 Everyday Ways to Love Your Neighbor and Change the World*

"There are times when a leader is so authentic, so real, so vulnerable, and so honest that those around do not just take notice, they take action. Albert Tate, as only a master communicator can, holds up a mirror for each of us to see and discover where we stand, how we show up, and what part we play in moving all of us toward a place of redemptive reconciliation. This book offers each of us greater understanding of what divides us, what can unite us, and why how we love matters. It is a clear and compelling call for sisters and brothers together to step out and let our love for one another—grounded in God's love for us—be the restorative hope that we all seek and pursue."

—Tom Devris

"Albert Tate's heart is on display in this timely and necessary work. Born from the fruit of his love for God and God's people, this book challenges us to live the gospel in community with one another. It is a call to be what we claim to be: followers of the Lord Jesus Christ."

—Philip Pointer

HOW WE LOVE MATTERS

· ·

A CALL TO PRACTICE RELENTLESS RACIAL RECONCILIATION

ALBERT TATE

EDITED BY KATHRYN H. ROSS

FOREWORD BY LECRAE

NEW YORK NASHVILLE

Faith Words
Hachette Book Group
1290 Avenue of the Americas, New York, NY 10104
faithwords.com
twitter.com/faithwords

First Edition: March 2022

Faith Words is a division of Hachette Book Group, Inc.
The Faith Words name and logo are trademarks of Hachette Book Group, Inc.

The publisher is not responsible for websites (or their content) that are not owned by the publisher.

The Hachette Speakers Bureau provides a wide range of authors for speaking events. To find out more, go to www.hachettespeakersbureau.com or call (866) 376-6591.

Library of Congress Cataloging-in-Publication Data
Names: Tate, Albert, author.
Title: How we love matters : a call to practice relentless racial reconciliation / Albert Tate ; foreword by Lecrae Moore.
Description: First edition. | New York : FaithWords, 2022. | Includes bibliographical references. | Summary: "It is not an accident that racism is alive and well in the American church. Racism has, in fact, been taught within the church for so long most of us don't even recognize it anymore. Pastor Albert Tate, a charismatic speaker and rising leader within the megachurch world, guides readers in acknowledging this fact and reimagines discipleship by encouraging siblings in Christ to sit together in racial discomfort and examine the role they may play in someone's else's struggle. How We Love Matters is a series of nine moving letters, reminiscent of Dr. King's Letter from a Birmingham Jail, about different aspects of American and Christian culture. In letters that include Dear Whiteness, Dear America, and Dear Church, Tate calls out racism in the world, the church, and within himself and his reader. The book not only educates and enlightens, but also reimagines discipleship in a way that flips the church on its head. It looks to the life of our savior Jesus Christ as less of a blueprint for how we should live and more as a clear instruction manual for how we need to treat and love one another as siblings and neighbors, regardless of differences like skin color, culture, language, or beliefs. Tate believes that the only way to make change is by telling the truth about where we are-relationally, internally, and spiritually. How We Love Matters is an exposition of relevant Biblical truth, a clarion call for all believers to examine how they see and understand each other, and it is a way forward toward justice, reconciliation, and healing"—Provided by publisher.
Identifiers: LCCN 2021041706 | ISBN 9781546000532 (hardcover) | ISBN 9781546000556 (ebook)
Subjects: LCSH: Love—Religious aspects—Christianity. | Race relations—Religious aspects—Christianity. | Reconciliation—Religious aspects—Christianity.
Classification: LCC BV4639 .T38 2022 | DDC 241/.4—dc23
LC record available at https://lccn.loc.gov/2021041706

ISBN: 9781546000532 (hardcover), 9781546000556 (ebook)

Printed in the United States of America

LSC-C

Printing 1, 2021

To the love of my life, my amazing wife, LaRosa, thank you so much for loving me so well all these years. Thanks for loving me and encouraging me to be the husband, the dad, the man, the pastor, and now the author that I get to be today. I am who I am because of you, and I am forever thankful. And thanks again for paying that $500 cell phone bill back in 2001.

To my amazing children, Zoe, Bethany, Isaac, and Micah, Daddy loves you more than you could ever imagine. I hope and pray that the words of these pages will pale in comparison to my presence in your life. You all by far are the greatest story I will ever tell and the greatest sermon that I'll ever preach.

CONTENTS

FOREWORD

During a hot summer week years ago, I found myself trying to be a model husband, father, leader, and follower of Christ. So like most good-ole American Christians I took my family to a Christian camp. It was a mix of many things I hate—the outdoors, bugs, snakes, heat, and mostly acoustic guitars and Christian songs I don't know. My family was one of the few families of color and I found myself struggling.

It wasn't that I hadn't been around mostly white brothers and sisters in Christ before. It wasn't that I was unaccustomed to places where there was very little Fred Hammond and a lot of Hillsong. It was that I was struggling with the racial tension in America. I was struggling as a follower of Christ to find voices that could speak to my very real racial trauma yet still point me to a hope in the Scriptures. I just knew this summer week would be one where I battled cynicism and grief, but as my grandmother says, God may not show up when you want Him to, but He's always on time.

Our speaker that week was Albert Tate. Immediately his words began to fill up my thirsty soul with truth and wisdom. I was not only hearing God speak through Albert—I was being healed. Then and now he has a way of communicating so that all listeners can walk away challenged and encouraged, provoked and loved.

There have been many conversations in my community about how much he has blessed us. His words in this book will allow you to see from afar what I have seen up close. He is a mere man, but he allows himself to be an instrument of an extraordinary God.

—Lecrae

....

CHAPTER 1

DEAR READER

9 MINUTES, 29 SECONDS

Take a moment to look at this time stamp. It's not quite ten minutes, but it's close. It's short for a commute—for a walk or a bike ride. Short for a film or an appointment.

But it's a long song. A long time to not know where your child is. It's a long time to be in pain and distress, to feel fear.

And it's a really long time to not be able to breathe.

Those nine minutes and twenty-nine seconds Derek Chauvin held his knee against George Floyd's neck stopped the entire world in its tracks. Everyone who came across the footage stopped and stared. It spread like wildfire across social media, popping up without warning and showing a man slowly losing his life in one of the most shocking, disgusting, and horrifying ways anyone has ever seen. Even more harrowing was the display of police brutality and racism—a Black man pressed into the ground while a white police officer kneeled on his neck, squeezing the life from him as he cried, over and over again, that he couldn't breathe.

As suddenly as the world stopped, it exploded. Protests erupted across the country and across the globe. People were marching for Black lives and calling for justice, reform, and healing. The scenes were fraught—and all of this while we were contending with a pandemic.

Let's park there for just a moment.

The year 2020 was marked by so many dynamics, issues, and concerns that many of us have never fully faced before and are still processing. The pandemic descended on us so suddenly and completely that we didn't have a moment to think as we adjusted to a new normal: One week we were gathering in buildings without masks, able to talk, hug, and be with our friends and family, and the next we were on lockdown, confined to our homes. People were panic-buying toilet paper until it was scarce; we were sanitizing our groceries once we got home and shedding our clothes to immediately toss them in the washer; we were buying masks, desperate to secure enough for our households and loved ones…I guess what I'm saying is, in 2020 the world was marked by so much uncertainty and fear—anxiety and exhaustion were at an all-time high. And then George Floyd was killed. And those nine minutes? Well, they felt more like nine years.

It had been a few months into this dynamic of lockdown and racial tension when my family and I decided we had to get out of the house. We'd been home every day stuck between news about the virus and the racial unrest, and we needed a change of scenery—to take some time away. So, my wife and I piled the kids into the car, and we went for a drive. We live near the Foothills in Southern California, which means that in just twenty or thirty minutes, we can head up into the hills and find a breathtaking natural scene to enjoy. After a little while we found just that; we pulled over in a little rest area where there was no one else around and got out, still wearing our masks, of course, to enjoy the view before us.

A few minutes later, two police officers showed up, parked maybe a hundred feet or so away from my family. They were just hanging out and chatting, so I didn't pay them much attention. A moment later, though, I noticed my nine-year-old son head back to the car and get into the back seat. Shortly after he left, my thirteen-year-old daughter headed to the car to check on her charging phone. I was keeping an eye on them, and all was quiet. When my daughter came back, I asked her what her brother was doing. What she said next stopped me cold.

"He's afraid of the police."

I looked around to where the police were still standing and chatting and then back to the car where my son was sitting nestled in the back seat. I made my way over to him, opened the car door, and poked my head in.

"Isaac, what are you doing?" I asked.

"Nothing," he said.

"Why are you sitting in here all alone?" I asked.

"No reason," he said.

"Are you okay? What's the matter?" I pressed.

"Nothing," he said again.

I gave it a moment, took a beat. "Son, what's going on?" I asked again. When he finally answered, he told me just what his sister had said: He was scared of the police.

"Why?" I asked, absolutely taken aback.

"Because I could die."

As a father, there are many times when my children have come to me with some fear of something that's either pretty irrational or just plain impossible. Usually in those moments I tell them they're all right, that what they're afraid of is really nothing to be scared of at all, and that they don't need to worry about it. But this wasn't one of those times.

As a Black father talking to his Black son, I knew his fear was valid and rational. I couldn't tell him to brush it off and not worry about it—that he's not really in any danger. When my son said those words, I immediately saw all the moments from my own boyhood when I feared the police. I remembered the stories my father and grandfather told me, about how the police treated them and how they, too, learned to fear them as young men—a fear they carried into adulthood. There is a legacy of this fear for many Black men—in my own family and families across this country. When my son told me what was wrong, it reminded me how early this fear starts, how it is both a tragedy and a necessity.

A necessity because that fear is grounded in the reality of racial tensions in this country and where they can lead. We saw the brutality with which a white police officer killed a Black man, the lack of remorse and the disregard for human life. Those nine minutes and twenty-nine seconds have marked my nine-year-old son's life. He has been changed by the reality of George Floyd's killing, and the killings of the dozens of other Black men and women, before and after George, at the hands of police.

I am the pastor of a multiethnic church in Southern California where the majority of the congregation is white. Even so, Isaac has been raised around so many ethnicities. He has aunties of all colors, friends of pretty much every race. We've created a diverse family around us, and my children have grown up in a diverse, multiethnic setting. But in that moment in the car, the reality of the racial tensions and dynamics of America were still there. Isaac was still a little Black boy, and he felt unsafe. A whole new generation has already been marked by the reality of racism—and that is why I'm writing this book.

It's past time to turn the volume up and not down on the realities of racial tension and dynamics in this country. I want my son and his generation to have a greater story—but to get there we have to talk candidly about our own stories and the racism and injustice we've faced.

The words that will follow on these pages are driven by this "why"—I want a better tomorrow for my children. I want a better world for the next generation.

STRETCHED BY JUSTICE

A few years ago, I was at a staff retreat. We were all milling around, settling in, and one of my colleagues was on her laptop. All of a sudden she called out, "All right, who wants to join me?" A few people raised their voices in affirmation and I, intrigued, asked what she was talking about. Well, every year Disneyland does something called the Half Marathon—13.1 miles to run (or walk). You can run for a charity or just for the fun of it—and let me tell you, I'm not a "run just for the fun of it" type of guy. In fact, I'm not a runner or even a walker; I'm pretty much just an eater/sleeper. But for some reason that day, I told my colleague to sign me up!

Next time I was preaching, I decided (in my hubris or folly—probably both) to let the congregation in on my new adventure. Everyone erupted in applause at the news, just as excited and enthusiastic as they could be. Well, the race was about six months away at this point, and I hadn't even begun preparing: no prepping, no working out, nothing.

Enter Justice.

Now, Justice is a member of the congregation, and this man is something else. He's absolutely ripped. His arms are the size of small cars, his physique is that of a bodybuilder, and he did, in fact, compete as a bodybuilder. Main point? Justice was in peak physical shape. As the weeks had been going by and the Half Marathon was getting closer, Justice was watching me every Sunday and, I guess, he was getting a little concerned. Eventually he contacted the church office to set up a meeting with me, and when he came in, we exchanged pleasantries, chatted a bit, and then Justice got down to business. He told me that he'd been watching me and hadn't noticed any change in me or my body (how could he tell? I wanted to know). He asked what I was doing to prepare for the Half Marathon, and I said nothing. I don't think he was all that surprised. So, Justice told me he has a gym, that he was a trainer, and that he wanted to train me for free to get ready for the Half Marathon.

I went ahead and took him up on it.

For our first meeting, Justice came over to my house with balls, ropes, and all kinds of exercise equipment I'd never used before. I was side-eyeing him pretty hard, and sure enough, those first twenty minutes were excruciating.

Justice had me exercising like I had never exercised in my life. I was sweating, huffing and puffing, out of breath, exhausted, and just about ready to give up and tap out. Around that time, I heard Justice say, "All right, Albert."

I thought that "All right" meant we were done for the day—that I'd completed my first workout and lived to tell the tale. But Justice kept talking: "Let's get the workout started."

I looked at Justice incredulously. "What was that we just did for twenty minutes?"

"That was just stretching," he said. "That was just the prep for the workout to come. You had to stretch your muscles first."

I shook my head in disbelief. That stretching almost took me out.

Friends, when I think about the next few chapters we'll journey through together, I think about the justice of the gospel and what it demands of us: Racial reconciliation will stretch us, offend us, go into our comfort zones and totally disrupt them—and just when we're about ready to give up and don't want to be stretched any further? That's when we hear Jesus calling, saying, "We're just getting started."

Over those months of training, I did not enjoy Justice, but I was thankful for him. I did not like Justice, but I loved him. I did not appreciate him, but I respected him and acknowledged that he was a necessary force and blessing to get me to the place I desired to go. This work of reconciliation ahead of us...you may not like it, but it will help us love one another better. We may not appreciate it, but it will help us respect each other better. This work makes us better so that we can, in turn, create a better world.

So, I invite you to be stretched—to be offended, to allow justice to be your trainer. Because the justice of God flows directly from the love of God.

Let's let justice stretch us through these pages, so that by the end, we're ready to get started.

AN INVITATION TO A STAINED TABLE

One of the most profound themes and visions of how Jesus sees mankind in the Scriptures is this: We are His family. We are the family of faith, the family of God. And in this family, there are ways we are supposed to treat one another.

Two words capture this family and who God is to all of us: Our Father.

There are huge implications here: (1) We have a Father, and it is God; (2) He is good and loving toward His family and children; (3) we are Our Father's children, and that makes all of us siblings.

I have four children of my own: two daughters and two sons. How my kids treat one another is a major deal to me. It matters that they are kind and loving toward one another, that they stick up for each other and protect one another. If how my kids act is such a big deal to me, then imagine how big a deal how we treat each other is for God.

So, yeah, how we love our siblings really, really matters.

Everything falls into submission at the table stained with the blood of the precious lamb. Everyone is invited to the table where we are reminded of these greatest commandments and how they must color every aspect of our being.

But unfortunately, most tables don't look like Christ's blood-stained table. Most Christians won't comfortably sit there. Instead, a lot of tables found in the modern church, especially the American church, are centered around whiteness as normative. What I mean by this is that whiteness is seen as both the standard and the norm in our nation. It shows up everywhere:

- For years Band-Aid colors have been made to match only white complexions.
- When the iPhone face ID was being developed, all the people used as subjects to train the tech were white, which meant that the ID initially couldn't recognize people of color or their facial features well once the devices were in consumers' hands.
- Until recently, emojis on our smartphones and tablets depicted only white people and skin tones. Varying shades of brown weren't even an option.
- "Americans" refer to white people, while all other Americans require a hyphenated term that includes their race.

While these things may seem small, they still drive my point home: Even the smallest aspects of life in much of the world, but especially in our America, are claimed for whiteness. Whiteness is the first thought, the default. It is the norm. And so, it makes sense that even our tables are centered around whiteness when they should be centered only around God and His heart.

The family table is one of every nation, every tongue, and every tribe, centered around Christ Jesus, but it has moved away from that. To get back to where we're meant to be, we must display godly sibling love, and that's why it matters how we treat each other and show up for one another.

Dr. Korie L. Edwards, acclaimed sociologist, professor, and author of *The Elusive Dream: The Power of Race in Interracial Churches*,[1] once said that "being diverse doesn't mean White people are not going to still be in charge of things." Through her research on the multiethnic church, Edwards became an ambassador for it, telling the truth about where it is and where it has the potential to go. Naturally, I've been incredibly intrigued by her and her research. Edwards found that while the value and vision of the multiethnic church are strong and compelling, the church itself has its limitations. The biggest one? Getting the whole family to sit and stay together at the table.

Over the years Edwards found that whenever multiethnic spaces of faith were cultivated, they were only as diverse and progressive as the comfort of the white members. Read that again.

Once the white members got uncomfortable about something, diversity stopped. And if the multiethnic church dared to keep going? The white members would eventually just leave. Edwards's research shows us that the biggest challenge to the multiethnic church, then, is how well we convince our white siblings to stay at the table to be stretched with us beyond their comfort zones.

This is not to say that I and other pastors of multiethnic churches want to target and push our white siblings. No, what we want to do is make the family table what it was always meant to be: a space for everyone to learn, to be stretched, to grow, and to know Our Father better.

To my white siblings who've found this book in your hands, I just want to encourage you. I want to encourage you to not fall into the statistical problem of leaving the table when things get tough. Instead, I want to invite you to lean in when it gets uncomfortable, to find comfort in the blood of the lamb and the love of your siblings.

This is my call for hope and healing. For a family table that's gathered to hear and learn from Christ. For us as a family to practice sibling love so that we may honor one another, honor Our Father, and so that we may make positive, lasting change for the generations to come.

CHAPTER 2

DEAR SIBLINGS

JESUS AND THE N-WORD

In my work as a pastor, one of my great privileges has been traveling to Angola Prison in Louisiana. Angola is a state penitentiary and is widely known as one of the bloodiest prisons in the country. It houses the most violent criminals you can imagine. Many of the men locked in there were convicted of rape or sexual assault, murder, or some other highly violent crime—and they're serving life sentences. In other words, many of these men won't return to society—they're going to eventually die in Angola because of the severity of their crimes.

With such a hard reputation, it will probably surprise readers to know that the prison is also one of the places I've seen God show up and move the most. The story of what God has done and continues to do in Angola is worthy of a book in and of itself. His work has been phenomenal and impactful, and I'm so grateful that I've been able to witness it over the years.

I was first connected with Angola through a ministry that regularly goes into prisons and supports pastors with leadership development.

I know, it probably sounds a little funny: pastoral leadership development in prison. Well, a few years ago New Orleans Seminary was invited to have a campus in the prison so that the men in Angola could earn a Master of Divinity and other preaching and pastoral degrees. The warden at the time, Warden Cane, decided to do something pretty revolutionary and let the seminary grads plant and launch churches right there in the prison. Over time, revival broke out. Angola went from one of the bloodiest prisons to the most blood bought.

Men were coming to Christ left and right, souls were being saved, and the gospel was spreading far and wide. As the years went by, my work with the prison led me to know some of the men on the inside pretty well. Going in, it's hard not to remember that any given conversation with someone in the prison was a conversation with someone who has seriously hurt and abused someone. Knowing that, I normally would have been filled with anxiety and fear just being around these men and knowing what they were capable of. But it's amazing how all of that fear and apprehension falls away in the presence of God. When we are all in the presence of our Lord together, worshipping and fellowshipping, the reality of their crimes and the worst of what they've done becomes irrelevant. I have to say that the men of Angola are honestly the freest men I've ever seen solely because of their relationship with God.

There's a photographer in the prison who takes pictures inside. He documents the services and sermons, and his pictures were put into a newsletter that was circulated among the prisoners with updates on local news, events, and stories. The photographer's name was Lee—this rather heavy-set Asian man who honestly stood out among the other men because Angola was filled with mostly Black, white, and Latino men. I don't know why Lee is in Angola—I've never asked him that—but I believe it was something particularly violent. Over my years visiting Angola and preaching and connecting with the men there, Lee became my brother. I'll tell you: We are so close. Whenever I see him, we always greet with a warm embrace and have a good chat to just catch up with each other.

So, one day while I was at Angola, Lee and I were having lunch together. Over our meal, he told me how and when he accepted Jesus as his personal savior while serving his sentence and about how amazing and serious his profession of faith was. It was life changing and earth shattering, but then Lee said, "But Pastor, I didn't know it was real until something happened to me."

I asked what he meant. So, Lee told me the story.

Some guys on the cell block jumped Lee one night. Using their advantage of surprise, they beat Lee up, but he eventually got the best of them. One of the guys was able to get away from the fight, and the main guy, the one who had apparently orchestrated the jump, was trying to get himself up to make his escape. As he watched this man struggling to stand, Lee knew he could take the man out if he wanted to.

"Pastor," he said, "this is what I do. I fight. I was so angry I could have taken him out. It would have been nothing to take his life."

However, as Lee was beating on him, as he saw the opportunity to easily and swiftly take this man's life, he stopped. He then stooped down, picked the man up, and sent him on his way.

Lee said that at that moment, Jesus became truly real to him because he didn't want to fight anymore. In that moment, Jesus and his faith took on a new reality because his enemy, suddenly and miraculously, didn't look like his enemy anymore. There was just something about the transformative gospel of Christ at work in him that made

13

this man and his cronies suddenly not look like enemies deserving of punishment. Lee said he couldn't understand it—but God.

Where before Lee could have and would have destroyed that man, a different response naturally came forth because God had changed him. His response and proclivity for violence had been transformed, and in that moment his enemy was just not his enemy anymore—his enemy was now his neighbor.

The power of the gospel is such that Jesus Christ not only changes our hearts, but He changes how we see one another—how we see our enemies and those who have done us wrong or dealt us hurts. Where before we harbored anger and pain, we are now filled with grace, just as Christ has grace for us.

∽✑∾

Throughout this book's development, I had a lot of ideas for titles. Some of them were pretty good and some were really bad. One of the really bad ones was "Jesus and the N-word." I can still clearly see the look on my wife's face when I ran it by her. Sweet, caring soul that she is, she was trying her best to be encouraging, but it was also pretty obvious that she was totally mortified and hoping this particular idea would not stick. Well, I got a second opinion from my best friend, Ricky, who, I must say, is a lot less loving and a lot more blunt than my wife. He looked at me and said, "Um, you want people to buy this book, right?" So yeah, "Jesus and the N-word" didn't make the cut, but I still think it's an important concept!

See, the "N-word" in this idea is "neighbor," and I just think that "neighbor" and all that the word entails is important to Jesus. I know we cringe at the idea of the term "N-word" being inappropriate, but I would venture to say that we think of neighbor love as something inappropriate in itself. In the gospels we see the story of the law expert hoping to test Jesus by asking Him what must be done to inherit eternal life. If you know how the story goes, you know Jesus simply steers him to the answer in the Scriptures: "Love the Lord your God with all your heart, all your soul, and with all your strength, and all your mind; and love your neighbor as yourself."[1]

In other words, the law is built on this faith and love that moves in just two directions:

1. A vertical dynamic where you love the Lord your God
2. A horizontal dynamic where you love your neighbor as yourself

Well, the law expert wasn't done trying to trap Jesus as well as justify himself, so he asked, "And who is my neighbor?"

I think we all have the capacity to be like the law expert—more than we realize or would like to acknowledge. Who is our neighbor? We want to act neighborly, sure, but who is our neighbor exactly? It's hard to act neighborly if you don't know who your neighbor is—the law expert has a point.

But if we really call Christ our savior, we know that argument just doesn't fly.

When we accept Jesus into our lives, we are brought into this transformative relationship that draws us close to Him. However, what a lot of us miss (or maybe don't want to acknowledge) is that Jesus and our neighbor are inextricably tied, so to be in relationship with Him is to also be in relationship with them. There's a direct impact on your relationship with Jesus and your relationship with your neighbor: They have to go together and they have to be connected. If one is separate from the other, you're missing a big part of what it means to follow Jesus.

All of the prophets and laws sit on these two truths, He says. They're one package: Love God, love your neighbor. The second direction is not an option for us—it is connected to the first and cannot be done without it. This is a cross-shaped gospel. Our connection with God fuels our connection with one another because it is through our love of Jesus that we're able to love our neighbors: those who were once our enemies, those who are hard to love, those who are different from us in every possible way.

Jesus is our ultimate source of power, and this vertical plug makes it possible to be connected to Him. Without His power, we cannot love, period. We cannot truly and unconditionally love our neighbors with a radical grace that only Christ can teach us because of what He has done.

If Lee were here reading over your shoulder, he'd tell you: Because of what Jesus has done, he no longer wants to fight, and his enemies have become his neighbors. That's how he knew his salvation is real, and it's true for you, too. What if the realness of our salvation was measured by the love we have for our neighbors? What if the true impact of our salvation were to show up in our compassion for our neighbor? I think we'd have tangible, measurable evidence of Jesus at work in our lives, and we'd begin to look more and more like Our Father.

OUR FATHER

When I think about the Lord's Prayer, these two words always stand out to me and shape me: Our Father. With just two words we're grafted into a family. We immediately become siblings because we have one father. Christ is inviting His family—His children, our siblings—to sit at the table. And, of course, with every family, there's drama. There's a mix of joy and trepidation at the family table, and honestly, that's just part of being a family—even God's family. If you look in the book of Ephesians, Paul talks about the idea of what God has done between the Jews and Gentiles:

> For this reason, I, Paul, the prisoner of Christ Jesus for the sake of you Gentiles—
>
> Surely you have heard about the administration of God's grace that was given to me for you, that is, the mystery made known to me by revelation, as I have already written briefly. In reading this, then, you will be able to understand my insight into the mystery of Christ, which was not made known to people in other generations as it has now been revealed by the Spirit to God's holy apostles and prophets. This mystery is that through the gospel the Gentiles are heirs together with Israel, members together of one body, and sharers together in the promise in Christ Jesus.[2]

You see, the Jews and the Gentiles were the epitome of people who didn't do life together. The Jews were the chosen people, the only ones previously included in the mystery of Christ. But by God's grace, those on the outside—the Gentiles—were brought into the family as one. Because both the Jews and the Gentiles have said yes to Jesus, they are now alive as one family in Christ.

My pastor friend Greg Waybright calls it "God's unexpected family." Going back to Ephesians, Paul says that all who love Jesus are in the same family: We are united by our love for Christ, and so we are united together—an unexpected family that is beautiful and expresses the manifest love of Jesus Christ and the diversity of all God's children. Of course, we have to be aware that as beautiful as this family is, it is marked with tension.

Paul reminds us that despite the tension and because of the gospel, it is our duty as siblings to no longer bring fight to one another, but to bring fruit.

BRINGING FRUIT, NOT FIGHT

As we think about being in a family with people who are unexpected and different from us, I can't help but think about the landscape of Christianity as a whole. If I'm being honest, I think so many of us are just tired. The landscape of our faith, especially the political landscape, has become so toxic and abusive over recent years that we are just weary. Because of this, I worry that many Christians have taken our cues from culture rather than Christ, so that when it comes to how we live out our faith at the table, we look less and less like Our Father. We bring more fight than fruit, and we show up in conversations and comment sections on Facebook and Instagram and everywhere else to pick a fight. My hope is that we will be more like Lee, that we won't want to fight our enemies anymore. I want my salvation to be real. I want our salvation to be real: no more arguing, defensiveness, verbal beatings, or blows. I want to see us bringing fruit to the table so that we may have a robust discourse about the issues of the day. But if I'm telling the truth? That's not at all what I'm seeing. What I'm seeing more often than not is a lot of fight, and no spiritual fruit.

This brings me to a passage I sit with very often: Galatians 5:22–23, the fruit of the Spirit. Whether you know it well or not, we can all use a refresher:

> But the fruit of the Spirit is love, joy, peace, patience, kindness, goodness, faithfulness, gentleness, self-control; against such things there is no law. (ESV)

As we look over the fruits of the Spirit, something always sticks out to me: This fruit is significant because it isn't forced; it just happens. The thing about fruit is that an orange is not working hard to come out of the tree—an orange is just what happens to a tree that is rooted in the soil and connected to nourishment. What if we were so connected to Christ that the fruit of the Spirit wasn't something we had to force out of ourselves, but was just something that happened? What if we were so connected to Jesus that kindness and goodness and self-control bloomed from us naturally? Whenever we had disagreements or disappointments or hurts, what if our natural fruit was faithfulness and patience?

When we talk about showing up with our brothers and sisters, specifically in the conversation concerning race, the dynamics of privilege, Black Lives Matter, Asian Lives Matter, Critical Race Theory, systemic racism, and institutional injustice, what would it mean for us to sit down and have these conversations from a place of love and understanding? What would it mean if we could bring the fruit of love and compassion to the table rather than fight and division? How might we be transformed?

We have to ask ourselves: Are we as people of God abiding in Him so that we might have peace? If the answer is yes, then why do we have so much fight?

For us to naturally produce this fruit of the Spirit, we must be rooted. The soil of our soul has to be seeded with the word of God. Like any good soil, it must be tilled and opened to receive.

Is your heart good ground for spiritual fruit to be seeded? Are you open to disrupting the places, experiences, ideas, and perspectives you hold that have become hardened over time? Can you become open to hearing and receiving the word of God concerning one another, the table, and the fruit we ought to be bringing? Is the soil of your soul open for God to do a new thing? Is it open to specifically loving people who are different from you (especially when you oppose their politics and perspectives), or who may feel like the enemy to you? Are you willing to be open?

I ask you again, what would it mean to bring fruit to your siblings and not fight?

CULTIVATED BY COMMUNITY

One of my favorite songs is "Open the Eyes of My Heart."[3] Based on Ephesians 1:18, the lyric that always strikes me is "I want to see You." What a request of the Lord! I believe that when we are truly connected to God, we develop a biblical vision of one another. When singing this song, we need to open the eyes of our hearts not just to see God but also to see our neighbor. In other words, we have to put down the cultural lens and the typical ways we see (or don't see) one another, and we have to strive to have kingdom eyes connected to a kingdom vision.

We must refuse to see our siblings as though they are anything other than our true flesh-and-blood siblings. What usually happens when you get into an argument with your blood sibling? Yeah, you're mad for a while and maybe you don't talk, but you eventually make up, and not just because Dad tells you to. You make up because the love you share is deeper than the surface. It is a steadfast love. What if we had such love for everyone around us?

Well, enemies immediately would become neighbors, friends would become family. A higher vision of love is achieved and made for the culture, and we no longer put limits on our ability to see, understand, and listen to one another to reduce our bondage in this world.

We will no longer ignore institutional injustice, systemic racism, micro- and macro-aggressions that hurt and wound.

This cultivation of the soil of your soul also happens in community. Don't get it twisted; you cannot do this by yourself. You have to be intentional about surrounding yourself with people, and specifically people who aren't like you! We have to step outside of our echo chambers and actually cultivate relationships in our hearts and souls that change how we love those who don't live, act, vote, or think like us. If we can love only those who are just like us, is that real love? Is that real compassion?

I can't tell you the number of times I've sat in conversation with my white siblings inviting them to see my burden and not be my burden. I can't tell you how many times I've carried the burden of having to defend my tears in the outbreak of racial injustice because white siblings want to logicize the type of death, the cause of death, and whether or not it was justified.

It is only through engaging in hard, challenging community that we can learn to see one another's burdens without becoming them, and then have the courage to lift these burdens as best we can.

To provide an illustration, there was a Black woman at our church who was in a pretty diverse life group. Let's call her Jackie. There was also a white woman in the group who had some pretty conservative views on race. We'll call her Lisa. Needless to say, Lisa had lived in a way where she hadn't carried the same burdens as Black women, especially when it comes to worrying about one's sons, husband, and other male family members and the police. Jackie was the mother to two sons and was married to a Black man, so the routine killing of Black men by the police affected her personally. At the height of the racial unrest of the summer of 2020, Jackie was carrying a burden that she often brought to life group. Now Lisa had a fondness for police. She had never had a problem with them or reason to be afraid. She didn't understand why Jackie was afraid and really struggled with Jackie's perspective. However, she was committed to stretching herself. She was in this life group for a reason, and she was intentionally doing life with people who didn't look like her or live like her. The soil of her soul was being cultivated in this small group, and she was doing the hard work of sitting at the table with God's unexpected family.

Well, as time and the group went on, Jackie and Lisa had an experience together. One day while Jackie was dropping her sons off at school, a police officer pulled her over. Now, Jackie just so happened to be on the phone with Lisa and was talking to her on speakerphone. So, when the police officer pulled Jackie over, Lisa was able to overhear their entire interaction. For the next fifteen minutes, Lisa listened to what she would later testify was one of the most devastating lessons that she has ever had to learn. She listened to the fear in Jackie's voice as she navigated her conversation with the officer. He was rude. He had a blatant tone: sarcastic, smart-alecky, disrespectful, and condescending. Lisa stayed on the phone listening to something she had never in her life experienced, and she couldn't believe her ears.

Finally, the officer left and there was silence. Fragile as Jackie was after that encounter, she spoke out: "Lisa, are you there?"

But Lisa couldn't answer because she was crying. She was nearly choking on her tears, unable to speak or do more than just breathe. When Jackie realized that Lisa was crying, she let go and started crying, too.

In that moment, Lisa saw Jackie's burden. She didn't try to defend it, explain it away, or rage at it—she just saw it and sat with her sibling in the grief and pain and weight of the burden. Like good siblings, Jackie and Lisa just cried together.

You see, to sit at God's bloodstained table with this unexpected family, we have to cultivate community and be open to seeing, listening, and hearing. We have to let the soil of our souls be tilled, even when the process is painful and uncomfortable. We cultivate our souls by cultivating our community.

I'm reminded of another story about a dear pastor friend of mine, Derek, and one of his congregants, Jason.

Derek is the head of a pretty diverse life group at his church. There were a few Black guys in the group, but the majority were white, including Jason. Derek is a Black man and they were doing life together and cultivating that community we've been talking about when COVID-19 hit and the church, like so many others across the country, closed down public worship. I can tell you from my own experience as a pastor that COVID-19 quickly created two perceived camps in the faith community: Either you had faith in Christ's protection from the virus and kept your doors open, or you were giving into liberal-media-induced fear and showing a lack of faith by shutting in-person operations down.

Well, Derek had already done his fair share of COVID-19 funerals, so he knew that closing the church doors was the right, and safest, decision for him and his congregants. The life group went virtual and had been continuing on as such as the months went by. As 2020 continued to drag on, we soon saw the deaths of George Floyd, Ahmaud Arbery, and Breonna Taylor, as well as all the racial tensions rising across the country. Many of the Black men in the life group had started talking about their frustration and grief concerning all that was going on, and so the topic was becoming common in their weekly meetings.

Now Jason was a gun-toting, Trump-loving, Black Lives Matter–hating, good old-fashioned American patriot and, needless to say, these life group sessions were getting harder. Soon, Derek received a text from Jason, and Jason said he couldn't take it anymore—he was leaving the group because he didn't like what his Black siblings were saying, and he didn't like that the church was staying virtual.

"You don't have faith or believe in Jesus," he told Derek. "These other guys hate the police. I can't take it anymore, so I'm out."

In response, Derek did something that I find really remarkable: He reached out to Jason and invited him to lunch.

When they met up, Derek asked Jason, "Are we doing life together? Are you my brother? Are we called to love one another?"

Before Jason could respond, Derek went on: "If all of that's true, then don't you ever pull this bull—— again. You're my brother and you don't get up and leave the table because you don't like some decision we made at the church or because your siblings are expressing pain and frustration you don't agree with. No. We sit at the table, and we have these hard conversations, and we love each other. So don't bring me this again. I love you and you ain't going nowhere."

After that, they finished lunch. And they kept meeting with the group. They're still meeting to this day.

Sometimes I ask Derek how he's able to do what he does and deal with it all: the accusations, the frustration, the ignorance. The last time I asked, I remember Derek looking at me with a lot of compassion and saying he can deal with it all because Jason is his brother and a good man, and he loves him. He, Jason, just has no idea what's happening in the world outside of him. He's been discipled by news pundits and conspiracy theories, and honestly, those things have discipled him more than the church. So, part of Derek's time with Jason is intentionally discipling out the racism that has been discipled into him. Then, he said something that really blew me away: "If I'm his brother and I love him, and I won't have these conversations with him, then who will?"

24

Friends, the soil of Jason's soul is being cultivated by someone who loves him enough to work through those hard places and help him see what he hasn't seen before so that he may become something he's never been before: a better sibling and a lifter of the burden his Black brothers carry.

Derek, Jason, and the group are still meeting and having hard conversations because they're committed to one another and to staying at the table together. One of the most challenging parts of loving one another well is staying at the family table when you want to give up and leave because the work feels too overwhelming.

REHEARSE THIS GOSPEL

In addition to staying in the good soil of community so that the fruit of the Spirit will just come out of us, we also have to rehearse the gospel. In Ephesians 3, Paul reminds the Jews and Gentiles who are tempted to give up on each other that they were far off, but God brought them near. They should have received death, but Jesus gave them life. As such, they are the benefactors of one of the greatest amnesty acts in all of human history: They were foreigners with no business being invited in, but God's grace brought them in. They were there by grace and grace alone. We are here by grace and grace alone. So, we cannot be invited here by grace and then act, live, and love our siblings according to our rights or their rights instead of God's rights. We cannot partake in God's grace and operate as if we got here on our own and by our own power.

Realizing that we're here by grace is what keeps us at the table. It's not us; it's God and His grace.

Paul prays that the Jews and the Gentiles won't be defensive but would stay encouraged to stay at the table and do the hard work of loving one another well. He reminds us that none of us deserve to be here, so we should all live by and give grace just as God gives us His love and grace. If we apply this truth to the conversation about race, immediately the conversation will change: We take the conversation about race and make it, instead, about God's grace.

OH, WHAT A FEELING TO BE LOVED

One of my favorite passages to preach is in John, when Jesus talks with the Samaritan woman.[4] I know, it's really a classic. But when we look at it through this lens of racial reconciliation and real sibling love, it takes on an even deeper meaning.

See, before we even get to the woman, Jesus calls out a cultural dynamic that has been at play for a long time: Samaritans were people who intermarried and intermingled, diluting the purity of the Jewish race. The Jews wanted a pure race, so they just decided to stop dealing with the Samaritans. They were so frustrated with them that they would avoid Samaria altogether: They would go around the land rather than through it, and they would just not engage at all. But Jesus doesn't adhere to that. At the start of this passage, He makes a point of going through Samaria and not avoiding it. He lets the disciples know that if they're going to follow Him, they aren't going to go around people, perpetuate cultural divides, and act like they don't even exist.

Jesus makes it loud and clear that so long as we're following Him, we will not live as if others are beneath us. If we're following Him, we must go through cultural divides, through cultural biases and prejudices, through self-righteousness and selfishness. We don't get to ignore people and make decisions based on our own bias, history, and experience. Just as the letter to the Ephesians calls for walls to fall down, we must walk through the debris of what's fallen down to get to the other side racially, socially, and culturally.

So, Jesus goes to Samaria and encounters the Samaritan woman. He tells her that she doesn't know what she worships. She tells Him that she knows the Messiah is coming, and this is the moment that stands out to me: "I am the Messiah you are waiting for. I am He. I am the one you have been looking for." Oh, what a joy it must have been to hear Jesus' words. Just imagine the hope, love, and restoration this woman has been needing, and she finds it all standing right in front of her in Jesus. She is so amazed that she takes off running through the streets saying, "Come see a man who told me everything I ever did! Could this be the Christ?"

It all reminds me of a scene in one of my favorite films, *Coming to America*.[5] In this particular scene Eddie Murphy's character, Prince Akeem, is so excited because he's just gotten his first kiss from his American love. As he's walking home through the alleys of New York he's singing at the top of his lungs, "To be loved! To be loved! Oh, what a feeling to be loved!" People in the windows above are yelling at him, hurling expletives and telling him to shut up, but he just can't help himself because he's just had this amazing encounter and has to make it known—oh, what a feeling to be loved!

I imagine the Samaritan woman doing something similar after she speaks with Jesus. She's just encountered a love she's never seen before, and it has changed and impacted her. To be loved—oh, to be loved! I think if she were to tell you how she was loved really mattered—that how she was loved didn't leave room for cultural bias to add to her burdens—you'd see how transformed she was.

Jesus loves her in a way that allows her to be honest about her burdens, struggles, and doubts. These burdens are lifted, and this love offers her something greater. Jesus loves her into her purpose, into something more than she could have ever imagined. Throughout His interaction with her, Jesus offers her healing and living water because she has been broken and abused—she's experienced less than what she was created for, and He sees it. He sees her burden and lifts it.

If only we as siblings would do the same.

Oh, what a feeling to be loved, to be loved by our siblings in a way that pushes us to be loved into our purpose and promise of our creation—our Imago Dei. Oh, to be loved beyond our racial divides and differences! But we won't get here by ignoring each other and avoiding each other. We need to see the divides and acknowledge them and the pain they cause in order to heal them. We have to go through Samaria because it's there that we will find and deliver healing and love.

I want to be clear: I am not asking white people to be the saviors of Black people. I am not asking Black people to be the saviors of other people. We all only have one savior and that's Jesus. But what if we followed His example? What if we saw one another's needs, listened to one another's stories of abuse and believed them?

All of us in this family have the ability to offer something greater: the living water, the power of the Holy Spirit.

At the end of this story, John includes an interesting dynamic. When the disciples come back and see the woman leaving, they have a ton of questions. However, they ask Jesus just one: "Are you hungry? We've brought you something to eat." Jesus' answer is pretty astonishing. He tells them, "No, I am satisfied. I am full."

The disciples wonder if someone brought Him something to eat. They ask themselves, How can He be satisfied? Then Jesus tells them that He has food that they know not of. The secret is that there was something about the encounter with the Samaritan woman that was spiritually and physically satisfying for Jesus. It filled Him. That moment of offering healing and love that was tailor-made for the Samaritan woman filled Him as much as it filled her. And friends? This same satisfaction is found at the table of racial reconciliation. This work of love is a satisfying work.

Jesus tells His disciples that there's food for His soul that they know nothing about—it's the first time "soul food" is mentioned in the Bible. So, friends, let us come to the table and love one another so we may feast on this original soul food.

HOW MY SISTERS LOVED ME

I am the youngest of three: I have two older sisters, Diowanni and Larissa, and I'm the baby boy. Growing up, whenever we took vacations as a family, they were always to church conventions, usually held at a hotel. I remember when I was about eight or nine years old we were on one of these vacations, and my sisters and I were at the hotel pool. We were playing around and having fun with each other and some of the other kids. Well, being the clown that I can be, I went to stand over by the deep end of the pool and started pretending to dive.

Reader, I cannot swim. I had no floaties. I had no business being on that side of the pool, let alone that close to the deep water. I normally lived in the three-foot section of the pool. Maybe one day I'll be able to dive into deep water and swim, but this was not that day.

So, I'm goofing off, pretending like I'm going to take a swan dive into the water, arching my arms and bending my legs, bowing my head, when this teenage girl comes walking by, sees me, and then pushes me into the pool.

I have no idea why she did it, but she did—just pushed me right into the water. Now I'm in the deep end sinking to the bottom. The water is closing over my head and I'm going down, and immediately my sisters are there. Larissa had seen the girl who pushed me, and she quickly runs over to her and begins absolutely going off. She tells this girl that I can't swim, asks her what in the world was she thinking pushing me in. She's about to beat this girl up—all the while, I'm still underwater trying not to drown. So, my oldest sister, Diowanni, jumps into the water to save me. She swims over to me, grabs me off the pool floor, and lifts me up and out. I'm hacking and coughing and all that, and I look at her in awe because she and Larissa have literally just saved my life.

See, my two sisters loved me well in that moment. They loved me like I hope we will love one another as siblings: that we will lift each other up, save each other when we are drowning, and fight those who dare push us down.

THE VACCINE

In the late fall of 2020, the vaccines for COVID-19 were announced. After nearly a year of work, research, and development by dedicated scientists the world over, a vaccine was finally ready to be released to the public. By December, the vaccine was rolling out to the most vulnerable members of our communities. I remember thinking that this was the first glimpse of hope for the end of COVID-19. However, just as hope was delivered, there was talk of a pause in vaccine delivery.

See, while the first vaccine was ready to go and roll out, it had some restrictions. Mainly, it had to be delivered at a very specific temperature to ensure it was still viable for use. Basically, it had to be kept at some subzero temperature, so all the companies, trucks, and pharmacies that would carry it now had to be equipped with special freezers to ensure the vaccine was stored properly for distribution—and not all of them were.

Thanks be to God that vaccine has everything you need to fight COVID-19, but it had to be delivered under just the right circumstances for it to be usable, and it took time for that to happen worldwide. I think this is an excellent demonstration for how we're meant to love one another as siblings. See, we already know love is the answer—love is our vaccine. But the temperature at which our love is delivered matters. Love is and always has been and always will be the answer. Jesus Christ has always been love. He calls us to love Him and one another and to hate indifference. In fact, He's very clear about what love is and what it is not.

The first letter to the Corinthians, 13:4–8, breaks it down for us:

> Love is patient, love is kind. It does not envy, it does not boast, it is not proud. It does not dishonor others, it is not self-seeking, it is not easily angered, it keeps no record of wrongs. Love does not delight in evil but rejoices with the truth. It always protects, always trusts, always hopes, always perseveres. Love never fails.

If we take and commit to loving one another in the vision provided for us in 1 Corinthians, it changes us and how we experience one another at this table. Like the vaccine, love does best under these specific circumstances, and it can take us a while to get there. It is a sign of spiritual maturity when your love doesn't look like what God says love is. We see Paul make the comparison himself in verse 11:

> When I was a child, I talked like a child, I thought like a child, I reasoned like a child. When I became a man, I put the ways of childhood behind me.

Like Paul, our love can be childish and immature, lacking under-standing. In order for us to truly love one another, our love has to grow up. And when love grows up? It looks like empathy, sacrifice, justice, and grace. When love grows up, it looks like Jesus.

As siblings, may we grow up in our love and let our mature love shape how we love one another. May our love grow up in Jesus' name.

CHAPTER 3

DEAR MISSISSIPPI

A HOPE DEFERRED; A DAY WITH DAD

Hope deferred makes the heart sick,
but a longing fulfilled is a tree of life.
—Proverbs 13:12

As a child, I got so much joy out of just sitting in the family car next to my father. Whether we were running errands or just taking an excursion out for the day, I always watched him and how he drove: the way he kept his hands on the wheel, how he'd smoothly shift gears, the command when he hit the gas, how he sat tall in his seat.

Early Saturday mornings Dad would wake me up and tell me it was time to go; we'd jump in the car, and we'd be off, just the two of us. I spent so much time beside him in that family car—picking up, dropping off, visiting friends, seeing family—and every outing was an adventure.

In 1994, my grandfather, a pastor we all called Reverend Tate, spent some time in the hospital. One weekend my dad said to me,

"Junior, let's go see your grandaddy." So we got up, jumped in the car—me in the passenger's seat, like always—and made our way down to see Reverend Tate. When we got there, we saw that he was sharing his room with another man. After we said our hellos and all to Reverend Tate, my father started gravitating toward his roommate.

Now, one thing about my father: He never met a stranger, and he never met a problem he wasn't willing to fix. No matter where we were or what we were doing, my father always made a point to get to know the people around him and to offer a helping hand if he saw they needed one. You name it, Dad did it all: picking kids up for church, mentoring the young boys and men in the congregation, talking to people in need of a listening ear and some advice, offering odd jobs to the neighborhood kids in need of some pocket change, and standing up each and every time he saw injustices in our community and the neighborhood. Part of this was Dad's good nature, and part was because Dad was a Vietnam vet and one of his postwar commitments was to be an advocate and always look out for the underdog. In all, my father was a good fit for the volunteer work he did with the local chapter of the NAACP in our home of Pearl, Mississippi, in Rankin County, and eventually he became its president. To this day he's a major inspiration for how I show up for the marginalized.

So, while we were visiting Reverend Tate, my father made his way over to the man sharing the room to strike up a conversation. But he stopped when he saw the man up close: He was bruised and beaten up, like he'd been in a bad fight. I remember being so shocked by his appearance—I'd never seen anyone so mangled and broken before. As my father introduced himself and he and the man got to talking, we learned that this man had been brutally beaten by the police. The conversation went on, and my father learned that this man had no lawyer or defense or any help of any kind—he was just brought to this hospital to recover, and there was no telling what would happen next.

Well, being the advocate he was, my father got on the phone right then and there with a lawyer friend of his and asked what they needed to do to help this man. "Take pictures of everything," the lawyer said. "All the injuries, everything." So, my father did just that. He got a camera and started carefully documenting every bruise, every scrape, every swollen place—and unfortunately, there were many.

While my father was doing this, the television in the hospital room suddenly lit up with a newsflash. It seemed to draw all of our eyes—a bright legend that read: "The Verdict Is In."

For weeks—but really years—a trial had been going on.

The celebrated Civil Rights activist Medgar Evers had been murdered some thirty years prior by a white man named Byron De La Beckwith. Evers was a young man when he died—not even forty— and he had been murdered in cold blood after weeks of threats. You see, Evers used his voice. The president of the Regional Council of Negro Leadership (RCNL), a civil rights and self-help organization, Evers had extensive training and experience in activism. He organized boycotts against segregation in every place from schools to gas stations, distributing bumper stickers with the slogan "Don't Buy Gas Where You Can't Use the Restroom." He studied law and became the NAACP's first-ever field officer in Mississippi in 1954, and he made extensive public investigations into the murder of Emmett Till. In addition to all of this, he was a family man. He married his bride and former classmate, Myrlie Beasely, on Christmas Eve, 1951, and together they had three children, one of whom is still alive today—a man of just sixty-one.[1]

So, this trial was the culmination of a thirty-one-year wait to finally, hopefully, convict Evers's murderer, a man who had openly admitted to and bragged about his crime at Klan meetings and rallies across the nation for decades. In truth, this was the third time Beckwith was on trial for murdering Evers. The first two times, the juries had been composed of all-white members. The first two times, the juries had been hung. But now? Now there was new evidence.

In moments my father was calling to me. "Junior, let's get down to the courthouse."

We said goodbye to Reverend Tate and his roommate, made our way out of the hospital, and jumped in the car. I can still see my father grabbing the steering wheel clear as anything, releasing the brake, and hitting the gas. We were off, flying at top speed down the freeway and streets of Jackson, Mississippi, to the courthouse.

When we got there, I was surprised to see there wasn't much of a crowd. Luckily, this gave us access to the courthouse, and we made our way up the steps and inside, careful to act like we were supposed to be there (because we weren't totally sure we should be). Inside it was packed with people and paparazzi—you'd have thought Beyoncé herself was in that courtroom with how many cameras and journalists were clamoring at the door, waiting with bated breath. We never made it inside the courtroom itself—the wall of bodies was too great. So, after all that hurry-and-go and adrenaline, we waited. At the time, it felt like hours. In reality, it was probably only about thirty minutes or so; meanwhile Evers's family had been waiting more than thirty years.

I remember seeing footage of an interview asking Beckwith if he'd killed Evers over the course of the weeks of the trial. Now remember, Beckwith had been bragging about this murder for thirty-one years. The question wasn't really whether or not he'd committed the murder, it was whether or not he'd be convicted for it. Still the interviewer asked him, "Did you kill Evers?" I remember Beckwith looked the interviewer in the eye and replied, "Did you kill him? Did you kill that nigger?"

As I sat there in that courthouse beside my father waiting and holding my breath, those words rang loud in my ears and that image stayed sharp in my mind.

Suddenly, there was an eruption from the courtroom.

"GUILTY!" someone cried. "GUILTY!"

It was taken up all around: "Guilty! Guilty! Guilty!"

The media rushed forward as the courtroom doors opened and Evers's family came spilling out. Abreast with other watchers and family members, journalists and friends, the crowd tumbled into the lobby: "Guilty!" Evers's family was crying, and I remember seeing them, or what little of them I could, with tears glistening on their faces. I saw tears and joy—I saw hope rising, spreading, radiating from them.

In my memory, I can see it all so clearly: their tear-stained faces, the smiles, the joy. I can hear it so loudly: those voices shouting in triumph. That moment of eruption—of celebration—was a disruption of a hope that had been deferred for a long, long time. I saw an exhale.

I saw an exhale that the deferment was finally over, and hope had finally come.

I saw an exhale.

I had never heard such sounds of jubilation before, and I'll never forget witnessing that unbridled joy of a three-decade wait finally coming to an end. Justice had come to Mississippi at last, and it was beautiful. I saw an exhale.

When my father brought me down to the courthouse that day, I'm sure he didn't know what was going to happen—what we would see and hear. But once that verdict came, I could see how proud he was that we had been there—how proud he was to have captured that historic moment with me.

As things were quieting down and we headed back to the car, I remember again watching my dad climb in, put the car in gear, and get ready to take off.

"Where to now, Dad?" I asked.

"To Walmart."

I looked at him.

"We've got to get these pictures developed so we can get them to the attorney," he continued as he peeled away from the curb. "That man in Reverend Tate's room is going to need all the help he can get."

Looking back on it all now, I see that moment as a picture of growing up in Mississippi, of navigating issues of racial injustice, of capturing a history with my father. It was a battle that had been fought for so long, and we were lucky enough to see the end and the victory.

The day was February 5, 1994, and justice was finally served in Mississippi. After three decades of waiting, hope had come, and the battle was won.

But the war? It's still raging on.

THAT BARITONE VOICE

Growing up, the epicenter of my world and my family was our church, Sweet Home Church of Christ Holiness USA in Pearl, Mississippi. Long name, great impact.

Sweet Home's congregation was not just a gathering of the community—it was a gathering of my family, both literally and figuratively. A good percentage of the parishioners were my relatives: aunties and uncles, cousins and friends. Sweet Home was a sanctuary. It held our community and our family together. It was a safe haven, a teaching and training ground, a literal home. And at home, one of the most impactful seasons was always Christmas.

My mother was the head musician and choir director at Sweet Home. Every December she'd work hard all month long to get our music ministry ready for the third Sunday of the month, our biggest event of the year: the Christmas Cantata. The Cantata was the jewel of the season. After extensive rehearsals and preparation, the Sweet Home choir would stand up and perform one of the greatest Christmas concerts you've ever seen. Our praise and worship was unmatched, the song selections inspiring, the celebration overwhelming. The place was packed every year because everyone came from everywhere to see what Sweet Home was going to do.

As a child, though, what really made the Cantata worthwhile—and let me just be real here—was these brown bags of goodies they gave out each year. Stacked with apples and peppermint and Christmas candies, that brown goody bag was honestly the most important pull for me Christmas after Christmas. Like, I'm sure the music was good, too—it had to be, under my mama's care—but that brown bag of goodies was just everything!

So, one year as the Cantata was approaching and I was eagerly awaiting my bag of treats, my mother found a beautiful song to add to the set list. The angels sang glory hallelujah, Jesus Christ is born... As the son of Sweet Home's head musician, I got to hear the Cantata songs long before anyone else, and I'd hear them over and over and over again. I remember listening to the billowing melodies and the harmonies, the way the tenors and the altos and the sopranos would meld their voices in beautiful unison.

As an homage to the old Negro spirituals, my mother got pretty particular about how the choir was to pronounce "born" when they sang this new song. As they practiced and practiced, she made it clear that she didn't want "born" to just be said; she wanted it to be presented with an accent that recalled our ancestors, the deep, soulful voices of the slaves out in the fields of the Mississippi Delta. She told the choir not to say "born," but "bone"! It was shorter, held greater impact. As a child, I thought it sounded so funny: "Jesus Christ is bone!" But I looked forward to that line each rehearsal, and its impact only deepened when Mama chose that year's soloist: our cousin Felton Hill.

Now, Felton hadn't grown up around the area. He and his family had moved from Oakland, California, and joined the church—him, his wife, Cassandra, and their three boys. Felton was a very kind man and a beloved member of our family, but what stood out about him most of all was his voice. Listen, this man's voice was one of the most powerful voices you ever heard anywhere. It was deep and smooth, grasping and soulful, captivating and commanding. Felton's baritone voice would reverberate throughout an entire room and stop everything. It only made sense for someone with such power to be our soloist.

To be honest, Felton wasn't much of a melodic singer, but he made up for what he lacked in melody with that deep baritone of his. I'm not exaggerating when I say it would completely stop you in your tracks whenever he uttered a word with exceptional feeling. So, when the choir was rehearsing, Felton said Mama's line like a roar of thunder: "Jesus Christ is bone!" I remember getting chills each time they practiced. When I heard Felton's "bone!" I would smile so hard and so big because it was just so heavy. It reminded you of the gravity of the reality: Jesus Christ—Jesus Christ!—came into this world and put on flesh to be among us, His children. He was bone!

Whatever Felton said, you just couldn't forget. And there was soon another time his deep rumble would stop me in my tracks.

It was another Sunday and some of the men of the church were having a meeting that was getting to be a little...contentious.

My father, as contrarian as he was helpful, had a knack for stirring people up. We were discussing Men's Day, a special Sunday when the church would focus entirely on the men of the congregation. We also had Women's Day and Youth Day, Usher's Day, etc. But on Men's Day, we celebrated the men: The men's choir would sing, one of the elder male pastors would preach, and we'd always invite a special guest speaker from the community to come and join us that afternoon.

At the meeting that Sunday, my best friend, Ricky Jenkins, and I were by his side, watching as my father offered different perspectives and ideas than whatever the rest of the group wanted. Now, don't get it twisted—my father wasn't contrarian just for the heck of it. No, what he was doing was voicing his unique thoughts and letting his views be known. My father didn't stifle his perspective, nor did he force it on anyone. He simply gave it room to breathe and space to be. So, when everyone in the church wanted to go left, my father often came up with several good reasons why they should consider going right. Some might say I inherited my own unique contrarian perspective from him, and, honestly, they're probably right.

That day in the meeting, my father had an idea. He had a close friendship with the Mississippi Supreme Court justice Jim Smith and thought he would be an excellent pick for that year's Men's Day speaker. In fact, my father was so passionate about his idea that he had put together a whole presentation to get Smith to be the pick.

To my surprise, though, the other men weren't really on board with Dad's idea.

In fact, they were pushing back pretty heavily, and tensions were rising. No matter how many good reasons my father gave for Smith being their pick, the other men shot him down at every turn. Despite this, my father kept countering each objection with another good point in Smith's favor. It was like a reverse game of Jenga: My father would pull just the right piece and the other man's argument would come falling down.

Well, while my father was holding his own and making point after point, the arguing went on and on. We couldn't come to an agreement: My father was so passionate about picking Smith, and the other men just wouldn't agree. Finally, that great baritone voice broke out and cut the tension in the room clean in half: "Because he's white," Felton called.

Once again, that baritone voice had captured a room and stopped everything in its tracks. I remember sitting in that moment and feeling the truth and the pain of those words wash over me: The men didn't want Smith as their speaker because he was white.

That was the moment it hit me: Sweet Home Church of Christ Holiness USA didn't have any white people in the congregation—and not only because white people didn't want to be there. No. Sweet Home didn't have white congregants because the Black church members, my family, didn't want them there.

I had never heard this said out loud before. It had never struck me before. But in that meeting the tensions rose high enough for it to be said, for Felton, with all the power in his voice, to say it. And most did not disagree with him.

What I would discover many years later was that there were two main reasons for this view. I want to be clear: It was never that white people weren't welcome at Sweet Home, it was that the church didn't feel safe with them there.

Reconciling what Sweet Home was to me with this new reality was harrowing. Because on Sunday mornings, Sweet Home was the place to be. Elder Willie Jenkins, our senior pastor and grandfather of my best friend, Ricky, was this amazing, larger-than-life man. He could go from soft-spoken to a raging high pitch of conviction in six seconds flat. I've seen Elder Jenkins reduce grown men to tears with the thunder of his voice. He was lit with holy fire when he preached, and he would unleash it on all of us, calling people to righteousness, bringing people to reconciliation and healing, consoling people in times of heartbreak and brokenness. Under his tutelage many came to the altar and were saved. Together with his wife he mentored broken families and couples until the tears would flow and vows were renewed. In short, our senior pastor was a force to be reckoned with, and Sweet Home, his stomping ground, was a sacred place.

Each Sunday when Elder Jenkins would finish a thunderous sermon, my mother, Connie Tate, would come in and lead the choir to sing before the whole congregation. I may be biased, sure, but believe me when I say that when my mother was up there, it was like our congregation had been out at sea, whipped and stirred up by Elder Jenkins's words, and she was our north star guiding us back to solid ground. You could find your way by her voice like a clear trumpet call in the dark.

After sermons we would congregate in the Fellowship Hall, where all of us would pass around some of the most mouthwatering food I've ever had the pleasure of seeing, smelling, and tasting: corn bread and bowls of greens, buckets of chicken, buttered rolls, pitchers of sweet tea and punch—I can still see and smell it all, feel the warmth and satisfaction of fellowshipping together with my family and the Spirit of the Lord.

So then, how and why, out of this space of faith, sacrifice, generosity, love, peace, and togetherness, could such words be uttered? "Because he's white." How could Felton, in his commanding baritone voice, say he and the other men didn't want Smith because he was white?

❧

As I said before, the church was not just the church to our community. It was also the training ground for the Black family, where we learned about city systems, community issues, racial systems and institutions around us, and how to act and live and be in these spaces. Without this training, I and the other Black youth of the church wouldn't have seen the world very clearly—and we wouldn't have known how to prepare ourselves for what was out there.

Cousin Alma Jean was in charge of Sunday school down at Sweet Home. Short in stature, huge in heart and compassion, and a tenacious lover of the Lord, Alma Jean was one of my first spiritual leaders and mentors in life. It was from her, too, that I first heard this warning: "Be careful. Don't trust these white people."

Looking back, it takes me a moment to ground and accept the fact that I learned to be wary of white people from my church. That part of my discipleship was a warning against and a wariness toward them. That my spiritual education came with a built-in warning, concern, and caution against whites.

Cousin Alma Jean also worked at Pearl High School, so between normal school and Sunday school us kids saw her a lot. Likewise, she was around to see us, the young Black children of the church, growing and learning and coming of age at the school alongside our white peers. We were on the football and basketball teams together, the cheerleading squad and various clubs. We were intermingling with the white children around us, being familiar with them in our innocence and naivete as children. So, Alma Jean would tell each of us, her Black cousins and nieces and nephews, what she told me: Be careful. Oftentimes she'd pull us aside and say, "It's great you're having fun and a good time but be careful around these white people. Don't trust them."

So, these warnings, which in all honesty I would call sanctified warnings, made me ask myself over time: Are my spiritual mentors racist? Are they prejudiced? Do they hate white people?

❧

While writing this chapter, I called my father and asked him some questions about the meeting that Sunday, what Felton said, and the warnings from Alma Jean. He listened and then he said something so profound: "Junior, we just knew what they were capable of."

"What do you mean?"

My father was soft but straight. "You're right that it's not that they weren't welcome, but the Black church is and was a safe place for us, and we didn't want our safe place to be disrupted or contaminated with evil."

I sat with that for a minute, and my father went on: "We just had to warn y'all, Junior. We saw you getting so comfortable around them, and we had to warn you because we just knew what they were capable of."

My father is not a very old man. His words are not echoes of trauma from a hundred years ago, or even eighty years ago. My father saw things he can never unsee not that long ago. He and the adults in the church knew what whites were capable of because they'd witnessed them firsthand. Now, this doesn't mean they could predict or pinpoint what a white person might do, if they did anything at all. All my father and mother, my aunties and uncles and my cousins and the church adults knew, was what white people were capable of, and that was enough.

They knew a number of stories from the '60s that would illustrate their point, but the one that sticks out most prominently in my mind happened to Elder Jenkins:

In the 1960s, Elder Jenkins and his wife worked for a wealthy white family. Elder Jenkins tended to their yard, and his wife was their maid. One of their sons, Lonnie, in just the third grade, was one of the first to desegregate Pearl schools, along with five other children. Being one of the first Black children to attend an all-white school in Rankin County in the 1960s—well, as you can imagine, it didn't go over well. Soon, the Jenkinses became targets in their community. The local whites wanted to teach Elder Jenkins and his desegregating son a lesson, and the harassment began. They started coming by the house all the time and throwing bricks and bottles and rocks. They'd shoot up Elder Jenkins's car and yell awful, slanderous things, shout "nigger" as they sped by. This was frightening and infuriating, but Elder Jenkins and his family didn't react. What could they do? Soon though, things escalated.

One night, the white boys firebombed the house. They threw a Molotov cocktail straight into the big window in the living room and shattered the glass. In seconds the house caught fire. Elder Jenkins, his wife, and their six kids had to scurry out into the night. Ultimately the fire was put out, but the message had come across loud and clear. After that incident, someone contacted the Civil Rights leaders, and both the police and the FBI showed up to the Jenkinses' home to investigate. Not much came of that, but the community and the Jenkinses' family and friends stepped up. Each night someone would guard the house so Elder Jenkins and his family could sleep. They sat on their porches with their shotguns in hand, ready and waiting for trouble but hoping none would come.

Another time, while Elder Jenkins was tending to his employer's yard, his eldest son, Charles, came along to help. He was cutting the grass when a group of white boys pulled up in front of the house with a pair of Doberman pinschers—these two great, big, menacing dogs with their teeth bared and hackles raised. Without warning, they sicced the dogs on Elder Jenkins and Charles. With nothing but his cutting shears to defend them, Charles stood his ground ready to fight and stab the dogs if he had to. This wasn't just bravery. Charles was just a skinny fourteen-year-old kid. He knew he couldn't outrun them. He knew he couldn't escape unscathed. So, his only choice was to fight back. Seeing that Charles wasn't backing down, the white boys suddenly laughed and called their dogs off. Still laughing, they left. Charles was only fourteen years old; this all happened less than fifty years ago. Whenever Charles tells this story, his nephew Ricky always responds in dismay: "Fourteen years old and white people were siccing dogs on you... they were siccing dogs on you."

I can still hear my father. "We knew what they were capable of."

When I remember these stories now, I can clearly understand what my father and the others meant when they said they knew what white people were capable of. But one other story reminds me that that's not the end of the whole story. I'm reminded that when we walk this earth with Christ, we are capable of so much more love than hate, of more grace than fear. There was another time shortly after the bombing of Elder Jenkins's home when those white boys came back. They were cruising through the Black neighborhood ready to do what they always did, taunting, harassing, shouting slurs, and spreading hate—when something unexpected happened: They ran out of gas.

I know, I know. It's got to be the most ironic, karmic thing that could have happened, but it's true: Those white boys ran out of gas in the middle of a Black neighborhood. Stranded.

Well, they got out of the car and started walking. Elder Jenkins and his sons were out front, watching. Now, Elder Jenkins's boys saw this as a divine appointment for payback. Like a pack of ravenous wolves, they watched as those white boys approached and started making their way over to them, only for Elder Jenkins's thunderous voice to break across the scene:

"Boys, bring me my gas can."

Confused and a little annoyed, his sons obeyed. The white boys stood together looking scared to death as they watched Elder Jenkins, gas can in hand, head to his own car and begin siphoning off some gas. When the can had enough, Elder Jenkins stood up, made his way over to their car, opened the fuel tank, and began pouring his own gas into their empty car. In the process, Elder Jenkins cut his hand, but he kept going until the can was empty and their tank was full. With a bleeding hand and an empty can, Elder Jenkins tapped the back of the car and said, "All right, you boys, y'all get on out of here now."

ᗡᙣᘓ

That Men's Day, Jim Smith came to Sweet Home. After that very heated meeting, when temperatures had finally cooled down, the men of Sweet Home came around to my father's way of thinking: It was the right thing to do to have the judge come. Though there were still several dissenting opinions, they came together in the end and decided to extend the invitation. So, this white Supreme Court justice came to the church. As he moved through the sanctuary, he greeted the elders with warm hugs and wide smiles like they were all old friends. It was like they all knew each other—and I learned later it was because they did.

See, in his youth, Jim Smith had been a teacher. In the summers, he would come into this very neighborhood and pick up each and every one of his Black students and give them a ride to summer school. That day, I learned that several of the Black men at Sweet Home had been students of Jim Smith. So, when he came, they were greeting an old friend. When he came to Sweet Home, he was coming home.

That afternoon after the service, we all gathered together in the Fellowship Hall like we did every single Sunday, Jim Smith among us. As we shared food and broke bread, I heard Felton's voice in my head. Not him saying, "Because he's white," no; I heard him singing that line that changes the former, that made this moment of fellowship possible: "Jesus Christ is bone!"

MY SLIP IS SHOWING

If it isn't clear by now, let me say it again: One of the greatest joys of my entire life is having grown up in Pearl, Mississippi. The pace and the traditions of my family have so deeply shaped me that I really can't go anywhere in the world without the first introductory words out of my mouth being "I'm from Mississippi." I am so proud to be from the state where my faith was developed and my foundation laid, where my community and its hospitality prepared me for the world. I just smile whenever I think about how lucky I was to grow up there in my double-wide trailer with my mom and two older sisters, and my dad when he wasn't on the road.

See, my father was a truck driver, which meant that there were long stretches of time when he was away, and I was the only male in the house. Growing up as the only boy in the house, I quickly learned that undergarments were a very big deal. I was deeply acquainted with girdles at an early age because I was the one who had to push and pull those things into place and clasp those hooks until they were secure so my mother and sisters could get on their beautiful church dresses, and we could head to Sweet Home.

Now, the slip was the undergarment that surpassed the girdle. No look was complete without a slip beneath the skirt or dress to ensure nothing was see-through. The slip brought security, modesty, and an air of completeness to the final look—all without being seen. In fact, the slip was never meant to be seen. If the slip fell out, well, that was a major deal.

The funny thing about slips, though, is that they…slip. Made from soft, supple silk, slips have a habit of sliding down the body until they're peeking out from the outer garments, and that was a big no-no. So, of course, a common question I heard growing up was "Is my slip showing?" In other words, is there something that should be covered now that's uncovered? And if so, will you let me know so I can fix it?

Well, as I write this chapter and tell my story about my personal journey with racial issues and justice, I have to make one thing crystal clear: I am flawed. I do not have it all together. I may be the author of this book, but I still need the author and finisher of my faith to help me navigate the various spaces in life where I fail and fall short. In other words, there are times when my slip is showing.

Though I am covered by the blood of Christ, though I am part of a family of believers and my sins are washed clean, I have to be honest: Every now and then, like a wayward slip, my humanity shows.

There is a book called *The Body Keeps the Score*.[2] Now, let me just say this right now: I have not read it. From what I understand, this is a book that kicks you into gear when you read it—that inspires you to totally change your life. If I'm being honest, I am not ready for that level of change or all-encompassing intensity—especially not after the year we've just had, let's be honest. I believe in baby steps for certain areas of life, so I know I'm not ready to actually read this book. Even so, the title alone has been impacting and changing me in ways I could never have imagined. See, this book is all about how our bodies remember and hold trauma even when our minds don't process it (or, more accurately, try to ignore it). But it's not just that the body "keeps the score"—it's also changed by the score over time. This means that trauma we experienced, trauma experienced by our parents, our grandparents, and so on, is all present in our bodies and it affects us. This book offers us an understanding of how these effects impact us, and then gives us advice and steps on how to work with our bodies to process trauma better. Like I said, it's intense and I'm not yet ready to read it, but the premise is already so transformative.

In recent years, so much research has been done by various therapists and psychologists to uncover the truth about trauma and what it does to our bodies. When something happens to us, even if we think it didn't affect us much or we've decided to push it away and forget about it, the reality is that the body takes note of it—takes note of everything. We physically hold on to what happens to us in life, even if we don't know we're doing so. So, everything that happens to us is recorded— our bodies hold it and they truly do keep score.

The first time someone called me "nigger," I was in the seventh grade.

I was twelve or thirteen and I was just coming into my confidence, finding out who I was and who I wanted to be. I wasn't popular, I was first tenor in the choir; I was just figuring it all out. Well, there was this kid in my class named Joe. As far as twelve- and thirteen-year-olds go, the guy was tough. He stood a couple feet taller than me; I think he played football (and if he didn't, he could have), and he was strong. Normally, Joe was a pretty nice kid. I'd never had any run-ins with him before, and to my knowledge he wasn't a bully or anything, but one day he just came for me. I don't know why, but he came for me.

I remember I was standing in the hallway at school when Joe suddenly came up to me, sneering, and said something to the effect of "You ain't nothing but an old nigger."

I looked at him and everything seemed to stop.

Before I knew it, I had punched Joe straight in the mouth, sent my knee into his stomach, and as he was doubling over, my elbow was about to collide with his chin. I was livid; I was ready to give Joe the whupping of his life. As Joe was hitting the floor, I woke up from my daydream and realized I was still standing there. Hadn't moved. It'd been maybe ten seconds since he said what he said: "You ain't nothing but an old nigger."

In that moment my mind broke out of my anger and disbelief and gave me a pretty grounding message: "Albert, you don't know how to fight!" As I considered this, my mind kept going: "Joe is bigger and stronger than you! You have never even been in a fight, but he probably has! You don't know what you're doing, and now is not the time to figure it out!"

I was ill prepared to handle that moment. What I wanted to do was light into Joe and send him home crying, but I knew I really couldn't do anything. When Joe called me a nigger that day, all I could do was look back at that white boy and take his words.

What I would soon learn over the years was that that moment didn't just dissolve like my fantasies of fighting. No, that moment went somewhere. It didn't just go away—my body held on to it. All the shock and adrenaline, all that pain and anger and helplessness still lives in me, and I can remember it as clearly as if it happened yesterday. What

I'm trying to stress is, the body truly does keep score. And for Black people in this country? There's so much to record.

In America, there's something that happens to many Black people that most people just don't know about. In order for us to stay safe, out of danger, and to feel protected, we learn from a very young age to perform so as not to disrupt the flow of, or get in the way of, white people. This is called code switching. Throughout my life, I have had to be a different person when in the presence of white men and women. If I went on a job interview with a white male, you best believe I did everything in my power to make that man comfortable with me. Why? So that he was disarmed and wouldn't feel threatened by the thing he believes Black people to be: the drug dealer, the gang member, the rapper, the threat, the thug, the foe—not the friend. So, code switching is done to make white people feel safe. If we aren't careful, we can find ourselves perpetually performing to keep white men and women feeling safe.

In 2019, the *Harvard Business Review* published an article called "The Costs of Code-Switching"[3] by Courtney L. McCluney, Kathrina Robotham, Serenity Lee, Richard Smith, and Myles Durkee. In it, they talk about a viral 2012 video of President Barack Obama in which he entered the locker room of the U.S. men's Olympic basketball team and immediately put on a clear display of code switching. In the video, there's a very stark difference in how Obama greets the white assistant coach (a polite handshake) and how he greets Black NBA player Kevin Durant (they clasp hands and do a familiar, brotherly half hug). The *HBR* goes on to identify Obama's actions as code switching, which they describe as "a strategy for Black people to successfully navigate interracial interactions and has large implications for their well-being, economic advancement, and even physical survival." It says that code switching involves "adjusting one's style of speech, appearance, behavior, and expression in ways that will optimize the comfort of others in exchange for fair treatment, quality service, and employment opportunities."

Well, like Obama and many other Black people, I've often practiced code switching. In fact, it has become a common part of my life. As a Black man, I must be very sensitive and cautious about how I show up in spaces, and if I'm honest, this is especially true when white women are present. Because there are moments in our history when making white women feel unsafe can be the difference between life and death.

On August 28, 1955, fourteen-year-old Emmett Till was brutally murdered. Four days prior, he had been accused of flirting with a white woman, Carolyn Bryant, while patronizing her general store with his cousins. Allegedly, he had whistled at her, grabbed her, followed her behind the store counter, and made vulgar remarks to her. When her husband, Roy Bryant, found out, he and his half brother went after Emmett and kidnapped him from his uncle's home. Emmett was from Chicago and was only visiting family that summer in Mississippi—those men tracked him down, abducted him, and for the next several hours we can only guess what horrors they inflicted on him. Three days after his disappearance, Emmett's body was recovered from the Tallahatchie River, beaten and mutilated beyond recognition.

In 2018, six decades later, author Tim Tyson revealed in his book *The Blood of Emmett Till*[4] that Bryant later recanted her story and admitted that she had lied—Emmett had done nothing to her. No one has ever done time for his murder.

If you need a more modern example, I've got you covered: Something happened in 2020 in Central Park that involved a Black man and a woman who soon became known as "Central Park Karen." Her real name is Amy Cooper and it went down like this: On a Monday morning, Amy Cooper was walking her dog while Christian Cooper (a Black man; no relation) was bird-watching in the wooded area of Central Park known as the Ramble. They got into a dispute because Ms. Cooper's dog was unleashed (which goes against the rules of the Ramble), and Mr. Cooper asked her politely to leash him. What ensued was a bizarre video Christian Cooper recorded (for evidence, just in case) of Ms. Cooper in which she called the police and frantically told them Christian was threatening her and her dog. In the video, her voice escalates, and she sounds more and more distressed and hysterical while Christian stands there silently watching and recording. Of course, the video went viral, and it came in handy when a police investigation was inevitably launched because of Ms. Cooper's claims. "I videotaped it because I thought it was important to document things," Christian Cooper was quoted telling CNN. "Unfortunately, we live in an era with things like Ahmaud Arbery, where Black men are seen as targets. This woman thought she could exploit that to her advantage, and I wasn't having it."[5]

Imagine where Emmett Till might have been if smartphones existed in the '50s. Would the evidence have mattered? I don't know the answer to that question, but I do know that so long as the white people around me don't feel safe, I am not safe.

A few years ago, I was in a meeting with some colleagues. There were three of us: me, a white man, and a white woman. We were representatives of three different organizations, and our meeting was to accomplish a task that, at the end of the day, would have a significant impact on each of our organizations and where we stood in them. To tell the truth, the task at hand should have been easy even though the stakes were high, but it was proving to be more and more of a challenge the longer we were at it. So, we were all in this room together talking and negotiating, navigating the nuances of the conversation, but things just kept getting more difficult. At one point, the white woman seemed to assume she had some support for her perspective, but we soon learned she really didn't. As we were all talking, it became clear that I was opposed to her position, and so the main tension of the meeting was rising between us as we went on. What she didn't know, however, was that the other man, the white man, had switched sides while we were talking, and where before he had supported her position, he was now supporting mine. As the conversation continued and became more heated, the white woman said something that triggered me so completely that it shook up my engagement with this meeting as a whole and made me want to leave the room entirely.

She said, "I no longer feel safe in this conversation. I no longer feel safe talking about this anymore."

Now, if I'm assuming the best, I think that all she meant was that she didn't want to talk about this issue anymore because she was in the minority position and she was frustrated. But if I'm being honest? When I heard this white woman say, "I don't feel safe," I was immediately transported back to Sunday school with Alma Jean, to my father's words, to the impact of Emmett Till's story.

Look, I know what you may be thinking: That's a stretch. It's hyperbole at best to even equate these things. But as a Black man hearing a white woman say she does not feel safe, I tapped into my training all those years ago at Sweet Home where I'd been taught, discipled, and raised to set off alarm bells, proceed with caution, and ideally get out of the room and her presence. In short: If a white woman says she doesn't feel safe, then I'm no longer safe.

My slip is showing.

I refuse to be in a meeting alone with her ever again. Her words reshaped our relationship, and we have not worked together since.

Because if she's not safe, I'm not safe, and we live under a system where she gets the benefit of the doubt and I get the penalty of death just based on her accusation.

That may sound like too much, be too hard. But if you still think it's an exaggeration, I will say, tell that to Emmett Till's mother.

At this point in my life, I'd love to believe that I'm spiritually mature enough to no longer be affected by what's happened in America, let alone in Mississippi. I'd love to say that I've now seen so much and accomplished so much that the horrors I've written about aren't even real issues anymore. I want to believe that my holiness and pursuit of God have helped me overcome these wounds and I wish that I, like many others, could say those terrors could only happen in the South. I'm a grown man now. I live in sunny, diverse California and I pastor a thriving multiethnic church. These Mississippi wounds are deep in the past. But try as I might to believe it, it's just not true. No matter where I am in this country, even here in California, I remember the words of my father and Alma Jean: We knew what they were capable of.

Is that fair? Right? Is it even godly? Probably not. But it's honest. I still feel the impact of those words to this day, the warning in the wariness, the insecurity I carry about whether or not I've done enough to make the white people, the white women, around me feel safe. For me, white people still hold so much power and influence because I know how bad it can get. I know what can happen.

Like I said, my slip is showing. All this time later my training still feels as strong and as relevant as ever to protect myself, my body, my life. My slip is showing. My humanity is showing.

I left Mississippi newly married and ready to work at a megachurch in Southern California. My wife, LaRosa, and I had been packing up to move for weeks and soon found we had way more stuff than we knew what to do with. So, on our way out we went to the Pearl Swap Meet with my mother-in-law to unload.

This was my last day in Mississippi.

Now, that day I had been driving back and forth between the swap meet and our place, dropping things off and picking things up. Toward the end of the day when I was on my way back to pick up LaRosa and my mother-in-law, I saw an older white officer with them, engaged in what appeared to be a heated conversation.

I don't really know what the issue was—some discrepancy about where a certain table was supposed to be or go in the swap meet, and the fee that went with it. But I pulled up just in time to hear this white officer tell my mother-in-law, "That's why we don't like y'all over here no way."

In seconds I could see smoke spilling out of my mother-in-law's ears. Her eyes lit with anger, she asked, "What did you say??" Before waiting for any answer, she cried, "That's why I don't like coming over here to Rankin County because y'all are so racist!"

I jumped out of the car and grabbed my mother-in-law before she did or said anything else. I knew I had to get her and my wife far away from this situation as quickly as I could. In that same moment, the officer looked at me and said, "Yeah, boy, you better get out of here." I looked back at him and said evenly, "Sir, we're leaving. You don't have to talk to us that way."

The reaction was immediate. The officer raised his eyebrows and came at me with a threatening eye and a whole lot of bravado. "What did you say?" There was something like excitement in his eyes. Like what I had just said to him was what he'd been waiting for. He came at me then like he was hungry to give me something, daring me to speak again. It was like I was the slave, and he was the master, daring a wily buck to step out of line. I glanced at my wife and saw horror in her eyes. "Albert," she said, "let's just go."

The officer was still watching me, and I looked back at him. I can't describe the rage I felt in that moment. I was a grown man now, not the little boy in seventh grade. And this old police officer was no Joe.

But something happened to me that day because of my wife's fear. Seeing the look in her eyes, feeling the anger I felt, I knew that whatever happened next was going to drastically impact the next twenty-four to seventy-two hours. By the grace of God, I looked back at my wife and then back at this officer. He was excited, daring me to lash out. I looked him in the eyes, and I swallowed it.

That was my last day in Mississippi. As I write this, I don't want anyone to think I'm some hero. Love and the Lord held my tongue that day. But that incident, much like that fight with Joe, still lives in me. The body keeps the score and sometimes, my slip—my humanity—shows. God is still healing me.

FLAGS DO FALL

As we close out this chapter, I'm reminded of one of the best jobs I ever had as a kid: census taker in 1990. One of my duties was to go door to door to find out how many people were living in each household, and this sometimes took me to some pretty rural backwoods neighborhoods around Mississippi. I'll admit that as a young Black man, the more rural the area, the more nervous I was. I would often get out of the car with great trepidation in these spaces because they were always decorated with a prolific landmark: the Confederate flag.

I'll never forget driving into a neighborhood and seeing a tag on a car that read, "Let's Go Back to the Old South," with a picture of that rebel flag. That day I got right back in my car and drove away. I had to guess how many people that household held because I knew that rebel flag paired with that idealism for the Old South could mean nothing good for me.

To some, that flag may represent southern belles and garden parties, big weddings, sprawling plantations, and southern state's rights. But the question is: Rights to do what? The Old South is when slavery and abuse reigned, and that rebel flag really means only one thing: the perpetuation of one of the biggest systems of injustice in American history. What's more? That is the flag of the losing side. It's flown longer than its cause, and in Mississippi, that flag has had a long, long history.

When I gave my life to Christ and started the journey to becoming a pastor, I got my GED and made my way to Wesley Bible College in Florence, Mississippi. The year was 2001, and there was a vote at the state level to change the Mississippi flag so that it no longer included the Confederate flag within it.

In that setting of Christian academics—remember, my classmates and I were training to be pastors and church leaders—there was a discussion about what to do with the rebel flag. This was my first time in a setting like this with majority-white class members. They were my classmates, but they were also my friends—my brothers and sisters in Christ. So, to sit in that room and have the class discuss and debate this flag that represents so much hate and racism was disorienting to say the least. To me, it was a total no-brainer. But my white classmates? They were vehemently in support of the flag, basing their arguments on state's rights and their white heritage.

It honestly reminded me of a clip from an episode of the *Golden Girls* spin-off *The Golden Palace* that aired in 1992. In it, Don

Cheadle plays Roland Wilson, a worker in Blanche Devereaux's (Rue McClanahan) hotel who has an issue when she decides to hang a Confederate flag in the hotel lobby. While Wilson sees the issue with the rebel flag and the racism it represents, Blanche sees it only as a reminder of "wonderful family memories."[6]

Like Blanche, my classmates were in favor of the flag because it represented wonderful family memories. But unlike Blanche in the rest of the episode, they refused to be taught the full story behind the flag and how harmful it was to their Black classmate.

For me, something began to crystallize at that moment. I remember appealing to the class, saying, "Does it not matter what your white heritage did to my Black heritage? Can you not see that to celebrate your flag is to celebrate my oppression?"

What really gets me is that we were all in that class sitting under God's word together. My classmates called me their brother, told me they loved me, prayed for me—yet they were holding fast to this symbol that celebrated my oppression.

"You don't get to love me in whatever way is most comfortable to you," I told them. This is the flag of slavery, oppression, and injustice. If the South had won and that flag was flying in victory? I wouldn't have even been able to be in that classroom disagreeing with them. Yet, these white students said they loved Jesus, they loved me, and they also loved that flag. How?

I told them, that's not love. That's not love and we, more than anyone, should know that how we love matters.

Fast forward to June 2020 when the flag was once again up for debate, but this time with passionate opposition. Following the murders of George Floyd, Ahmaud Arbery, Breonna Taylor, and so many others, we were making our voices heard: This flag must come down.

Mississippi was one of the few southern states still clinging to it.

In the summer of 2020, after boycotts and protests, after businesses and organizations that once backed the flag aligned themselves against it and pulled their support, the political leaders of Mississippi finally got together and voted to bring the rebel flag down.

My good friend and fellow pastor, Chip Henderson, and I were texting on the day of the vote. Chip pastors the largest church in all of Mississippi, Pinelake Church. He and his majority-white congregation have been taking steps to ensure that their church reflects the fullness of Christ and the gospel. With his allyship, Chip and I have become prayer partners against outdated legislatures, and we'd been praying over that flag.

Well, that day people gathered to await that vote. Socially distanced and masked, waiting and praying, they waited for that vote to come down. I'll never forget Chip sending me a text when the vote was announced.

"Albert, we did it. We did it. The flag is coming down."

So, that's the story of Mississippi.

Mississippi, I love you. On your soil I've cried many tears, danced many dances, had many joys, and built the foundation of my faith. You are the place where lives have been taken and bodies have been bruised and broken, and you are also the place where I've been surprised by the investments and generosity of whites and overwhelmed by the grace and forgiveness of Blacks.

Mississippi, you have held the power of the church, you have been the home of the Black church that raised me, and you have made me the man that I am today.

Here at the end of this chapter, I want to emphasize that Mississippi teaches us all that hope may be deferred, delayed, but not denied. Flags do fall. Whether you have to siphon off gas in your own tank to put it in someone else's and hurt yourself in the process, or you have to work through bias and racism to give a shot to someone you don't think deserves it, the only way we can overcome, and the only way we love one another well, is by acknowledging the truth declared by Cousin Felton when I was a child: "Jesus Christ is bone!"

And because He was born, that changes how we love one another.

CHAPTER 4

DEAR WHITENESS

THE DAY WE MET

When I was in high school, my best friend, Ricky Jenkins, and I were part of the choral singers. As someone raised around music, the choir was one of the greatest joys of my childhood. The choir was led by Donna McCommon, who was a fiery Southern belle and an absolute force. She could command the room with quick wit, unmatched grace, and love and passion, and the Pearl choir was—and I say this without (much) bias—the best of the best. Ms. Donna ran a very tight ship, so we were always on point. Being two of the few pieces of chocolate in the choir, Ricky and I always did our best to hold down the first tenor section with some gospel flavor, and needless to say, our talent preceded us.

Well, when I had my first competition, it was, in a word, magical. The singing was beautiful and powerful, and all those hours of rehearsal really paid off as Pearl presented a show that was really worthwhile. Now, we were surrounded by other schools and choirs, of course. Some of these schools were historically Black schools, and unlike Pearl, their choirs were made up of predominantly Black students. For Ricky and me, it was extra cool seeing all of our Black friends at the competition because, while our choir mates were our friends too, them being white and us being Black did come with some interesting differences. In other words, we kind of stuck out at times. It didn't matter most of the time, until that day at the competition: I was never more confronted with mine and Ricky's difference, our otherness, than I was then.

One of the schools we were up against was Piney Woods, a predominantly Black boarding school that pulled kids from all over the nation. Now, Piney Woods was good, too. In fact, when the winners were being announced, Piney Woods won in their category. I'll never forget the reaction when their choir's name was called: Kids were hollering, high-fiving, crying, jumping, smiling, and dancing. It was so clear that this victory meant everything to them, and they showed it with heightened joy. It was cool seeing our friends so happy, but watching them, Ricky and I knew that when it came time for Pearl's win, we would show them up. If they could turn up over a win, we could, too—and we'd do it bigger, louder, and prouder.

Of course, when winners were being announced in our category, Pearl swept the board. We won, and immediately Ricky and I jumped up ready to high-five, fist-bump, and do a little dance with our classmates. But before we even made contact, we stopped and looked around. No one else in our choir was standing. Everyone was just sitting there looking like they were struggling to even clap as they brought their hands together softly and politely, like we were at a golf tournament or something. Ricky and I sat down awkwardly, suddenly stifled. We joined in with their subdued pats that passed as applause. Embarrassed and confused, we noticed our white classmates watching us with a mixture of pity and confusion.

It strikes me now that the way they were looking at us is how they looked at Piney Woods: They were watching uncomfortably, as if to say, "What are you doing? What is that behavior? How untrained. How unprofessional." They looked as if they were witnessing something out of control and unrefined.

At the time, I couldn't define what I experienced. But I remember how it felt: awkward and embarrassing, like Ricky and I were suddenly under a harsh and unfriendly spotlight that exposed all our flaws.

We quickly learned to acclimate to the culture around us, suppressing our outward joy for a more refined response. Pearl's reaction clearly said, "Of course our choir was going to win. Of course, they would announce our name. We aren't surprised by this, so a subtle clap that shows that things turned out as we already knew they would is all that's needed." Our classmates' reaction (or lack thereof) translated to a clear and simple message: "Do not celebrate. It is unprofessional to get emotional. Don't act like this is your first time here. We are better than that."

In that moment I was faced with something I wouldn't understand or fully recognize for another twenty years. I was given a message about the white standard around me loud and clear—that I was expected to conform and acclimate because whiteness is the standard. It's hard to explain, but it was just seeing how they responded to the Black kids who celebrated with such joy and emotion; they were embarrassed, they looked down on them and their enthusiasm. I interpreted it this way: Unrestrained emotion was "us" and stoicism was "them." And the thing is, it was all so innocent. It wasn't that these differences in reaction were oppressive, but it was the response to them and the feeling that accompanied them that affected me: Piney Woods' reaction was unacceptable, while Pearl's—minus me and Ricky—was appropriate. At the time, I just felt embarrassed and out of place. But now, as

I look back over my life, I know how the role of whiteness has shaped my experiences—and that was the first time I noticed it, noticed you.

I didn't know your name yet or the role you would invariably play in my future, but that was the day we met. I didn't even know the role you had been playing in my past. I had seen you before in different places and times. I had felt you and your influence. But I didn't know you and we hadn't properly met until that day at the choir competition. I met whiteness for the first time.

Now, some of you may be thinking this whole story is a stretch. That what happened at that competition wasn't racism or the result of white supremacy. It was just a different response to good news, and you may be thinking I'm making it way too deep. But for my younger self? For me navigating white spaces as a young Black boy? It showed me what whiteness behaved like, how whiteness responded, and how I had to be and act if I were to adjust to the whiteness around me—and it's everywhere.

During that choir competition and throughout my life, I was reading the story of whiteness, but I was never told it. I saw it in media and literature—the blond-haired, blue-eyed Barbie dolls my sisters had, the flesh-toned Band-Aids that matched only white skin tones, the depictions of Jesus in Sunday school as a sandy-haired, blue-eyed man from the OC—someone as far as possible from the Middle East. Even now when I'm invited to speak at different places and I go onstage to preach, I am handed a headset microphone that is meant to be flesh toned but is clearly designed for a white face. Whiteness is the standard, and we are taught that from the moment we're aware. The sooner we recognize it and comply, maybe the easier things will be.

Now, I want to be clear that I know my choir mates didn't do anything on purpose. That day at the competition, no one intended to do anything harmful. No one intended to do anything steeped in whiteness. But if twenty years of marriage have taught me anything, it's that there is a difference between intent and impact, and we are responsible and must be held accountable for both. That day at the choir competition was just a glimpse, just a moment, in a lifetime of adjusting to the whiteness standard. Scholar Willie Jennings of Yale once came to Fuller Seminary and gave a talk on the "nature of whiteness," and it was there that I was finally able to name it. I'd seen it all my life, but I never knew its name. Whiteness now had a name and a clear identity. I knew what it was and what it looked like. I could call it out.

It didn't start there, and it didn't end there—that was just where I met it for the first time.

Before we move any further, I want to be clear: When I say "whiteness," I do not mean white people. Whiteness isn't white people. Whiteness is a standard held globally, but especially so in America. We see it and feel it in codes of dress, beauty standards, behavior, and even theology. Again, whiteness isn't white people. It is a system that establishes white as normative.

Because of whiteness, there is a horizontal tension between people of color as well. When POC are trying to be as close as possible to whiteness, racism erupts among us. Colorism in Asian, Latinx, and Black circles abounds. Concepts such as "lighten up the race," "don't stand in the sun and get dark," "cover your skin so it won't darken," "choose a lighter spouse to create lighter children," and "lighter people are more desirable as romantic partners because they're closer to whiteness" are rampant. Multiracial mixing and marriage is often met with pushback or disdain by older (and sometimes younger) family members. Prejudice toward Black people from our other siblings of color comes because we are furthest from whiteness and thus the lowest standard. It all stems from whiteness and white supremacy—the closer you are to whiteness, the better you are. The further you are from whiteness, the worse.

So, friends, if we're going to have this conversation about whiteness and its significance, we have to be accountable and responsible for its impact—on ourselves and on society. If we focus only on intent, we miss the reality of impact and the pain of what was unintended. When we talk about this idea of whiteness, we have to talk about the impact it has had on America, people of color, and our children, and, if we're not careful, the impact it will have on our future generations.

Whiteness has been around for a long time. It's been shaping the narrative of our lives and holding us to an unattainable, unrealistic standard. But the good news is that now that it's being identified, it can be taken down.

THE PURSUIT OF WHITENESS

Whether it's seeing the many famous paintings depicting Jesus and His disciples as white, seeing that each and every American president until 2008 was white, seeing that each vice president until 2020 was white, or looking at the major movie stars and celebrities since Hollywood's inception and seeing that there, too, the majority are white, the message has been clear: White is better. Whether this message was given overtly or subliminally (and honestly, the world doles it out both ways), this message is obvious and rampant. So, as a young Black boy growing up in Mississippi, I got the message early. If your neighborhood was white, it was better. If your church was white, it was better. If you went to a white restaurant or you did your shopping and banking with mostly white people in mostly white establishments, it was better. Whiteness is just better, and that's why it's the standard everyone and everything is compared to. In short: The closer you can get to whiteness, the better things are.

For people who are not white, this message that whiteness is better creates something called internalized racial oppression. It's the idea that nonwhite persons are conditioned to think less of themselves because they're living under this standard, and the only way to be better is to pursue whiteness in turn. For example, if you're going out for a job and you're anything but white, it's in your best interest to act as white as you possibly can. This is where code switching comes in because you want to identify as closely as you can to white people and their experience so they're more comfortable with you and see you as a peer. The more you "act white," and the more you endear yourself to white people in white spaces, the better your experience and your chances at upward mobility.

Now, I want to be clear as I say this: No one has ever overtly told me to "talk white" or "act white." Truth be told, it's not a message that has to be said so boldly. But because whiteness is the standard and is so prevalent in the world, but especially here in America, the message comes through loud and clear.

That day when Ricky and I sat down at the choir competition, when our celebration was cut abruptly and dramatically short, my pursuit of whiteness began. I had been given the message many times before, but this was when I recognized and internalized it. That experience taught me to sit down in my Black culture, so that I might acclimate to the white culture around me.

At Wesley Bible College, this standard really stood out to me in the worst way. We were learning about homiletics—the art of preaching and writing sermons—and we went through this whole program talking about some of the greatest theologians of the past and of our time. However, as Bible college was coming to a close, I noticed that we hadn't been taught about or exposed to any Black theologians, or any other theologians of color, for that matter. Now, this was offensive to me because when it comes to homiletics, some of the best preaching in American church history comes from Black preachers. And I'm not just talking about Martin Luther King Jr. No, there was E. K. Bailey, Gardner C. Taylor, and Clay Evans, just to name a few historical giants. Some of the best orators, exegetes, homeliticians, and preachers have been Black, yet in all of my Bible college education, not one of them was taught in class? Let alone other great preachers of color, such as Sung Shangjie (John Sung), known as "China's John the Baptist"? History is rich with theologians of color, yet I and many others studied only white preachers and theologians.

It became clear to me that the Black men and women going through Bible college and seminary who were only being exposed to white preachers eventually went back to their hometowns and churches suddenly hypercritical of the pastors and traditions that had raised them. All year long these students didn't see anyone who looked like them or the preachers who discipled them growing up, and that gave way to resentment and criticism. Their history was considered second-rate, and so they saw this as true and acted accordingly once their education ended.

Of course, I don't have to point out how harmful this is, not only on the Black church but on budding Black preachers and theologians. It exacerbates internalized racial oppression and seeks to eradicate the faith traditions that brought them up.

Well, this lack of diversity in the curriculum didn't sit well with me when I was in Bible college, so when I see it in seminaries and colleges today, I can't stay silent. A few years ago, I spoke to the faculty and staff of a local seminary. I remember watching them as I referenced their syllabi and their reading lists, and I told them Black families can no longer in good conscience send their sons and daughters to institutions that ultimately teach them to think less of themselves and where they come from, where they've been trained to revere only white theologians because it's all they know.

If I'm being optimistic and gracious, I would say this is all unintentional. Of course, no Bible college or seminary wants to teach their Black students to hate themselves and their faith traditions. But the message is still there, and it's all the more sinister because it's covert. When only white theologians are taught and studied, it says that white theology is better theology, that white homiletical preachers are better, that white ministry models are better. I mean, the evidence is there: That's why we have "theology class" and "Black-theology" class. The impact of the hyphenation is devastating: My culture and theology are suddenly made other, less than. And I fear this has taught us as Black people to live hyphenated lives and lean into hyphenated experiences: The closer you get to whiteness, the better you are. As we navigate these white spaces, we invariably learn what's good, what's quality, and what's best, and none of those categories feature us and those who look like us.

If you're still feeling skeptical or like I'm exaggerating or being too sensitive about whiteness, I've got a story to drive my point home. When I was a kid, I remember being with a friend and his mother and driving through a new developing area near my hometown that was clearly a place white people would be moving into. You see, Black people had been moving into the "white communities" on the east side, so "white flight" was happening in response. More and more white families were creating new communities and relocating to the west side, away from where things were getting too . . . diverse.

Well, south of Jackson, Mississippi, there was a grocery store that was the go-to spot for the community: the Jitney Jungle. In fact, there were three stores: Jitney Jungle, the Piggly Wiggly, and Sack N Save. Great names, I know. But Jitney Jungle was, like, the hub. Everybody went there. So, one day I was riding in the car with my friend and his mother near this new development when we all noticed there was a new Jitney Jungle—except, it wasn't called that.

"Jitney Premier!" my friend's mother called out. "For the white folks!"

It was the same store with the same stuff, but it was in this new white neighborhood, so to my friend's mother's mind, it got a new name, a rebrand: *Jitney Premier.* At the time we laughed at her words; it was funny. But she was actually giving articulation to a message that it seemed had been sent over and over and over again: new better neighborhood, new "premier" grocery stores for white people. It was a higher standard for the white people in this new white space, one that matched the standard of whiteness all around us.

It's a mixed message, too: If you want upward mobility and to win in advance, the closer you get to whiteness, the better your quality of life will be. Jitney Premier for the white folks! But even if you get close to that standard, you'll never belong.

I can tell you, though it probably goes without saying: No Jitney Premier ever popped up in my neighborhood.

MY BROTHER DARRYL AND MY OTHER BROTHER DARRYL

The great Bob Newhart had his comedy show, *Newhart*, that ran in the 1980s and early 1990s. As a kid, I used to watch it, and I just loved this bit about these three brothers. Every time these guys came on screen, their introduction went something like this:

"Hi, I'm Larry, this is my brother Darryl, and this is my other brother Darryl."

The gag, of course, was the two brothers named Darryl—two completely different, distinct individuals who shared and operated under the same name. It made for a funny introduction and a pretty big laugh on the show, but it also provides a framework for this chapter.

When we talk about whiteness, it gives way to two brothers—two distinct concepts under the same name. Whiteness creates these two brothers out of itself: white supremacy and white privilege.

Meet my brother Darryl and my other brother Darryl.

Now, these two brothers garner different reactions. White supremacy? It doesn't take long at all to get a strong reaction to it. Most of us reject it. Those of us who truly call Jesus Christ our savior especially reject it—we name it, we see it, and we know it's an ugly, disgusting, divisive thing. So, we deny it and repel it; we know it is not for our society and it must be done away with if everyone is to live freely together. White privilege, though, is more subtle. To be honest, white privilege can be pretty hard to see.

I want to stop and say that this is where I fear losing you, reader. This is the moment where the defense mechanism comes up stronger than ever before, especially for my white siblings. There's a temptation to think there are actually two white privileges: one that looks like the KKK, and one that looks like Karen losing it in Central Park. But at the end of the day, it's driven by the same thing—"white supremacy" means that white is the standard. A lot of people struggle with calling this brother white privilege because the name itself is so triggering. If I can offer an alternative, sometimes I call it white advantage.

Remember, friends, that I said much of our time together would be like stretching. We're working out with Justice, and many of us haven't stretched and exercised in a really long time. So, if the defense mechanism is firing off right now, I invite you to continue to lean into this stretch with me. What might the Lord have you hear and see concerning whiteness and the two brothers? Stick with me and let's find out.

Okay, so white supremacy and white privilege. One is easy to see, and we are repulsed by it, but the other? Well, we have to better understand and unpack it before we can really face it.

White privilege is less aggressive, harder to see, less overt, and easy to miss because it's a normal part of our everyday lives. However, if we let ourselves miss it, we also miss the opportunity to grow and disciple it out of ourselves. White privilege and loving our siblings well cannot coexist. If we can't see the devastation and abuse of white privilege, we'll never be able to understand one another well.

As we seek to understand what white privilege is, let's be clear about what it is not.

At my church, we have a Center for Racial Reconciliation where we invite all members to come and learn more about what racism is and how it affects our society. Part of that reconciliation is defining and understanding whiteness, white supremacy, and white privilege. Of course, as I already mentioned, "white privilege" is a phrase that immediately turns people off. They get defensive and upset, and they usually don't want to hear anything more. To get out ahead of this reaction, we make a point to establish what white privilege is not. To be clear, white privilege doesn't mean that white people don't have any problems. I want you to understand that it does not mean that white people have easy lives that are free from hardship and difficulty. My white siblings, you have had to overcome a lot to acquire and accomplish what you have in life. White privilege does not take that from you. I once heard it summed up this way:

"'White privilege' does not mean your life hasn't been hard. It just means your skin tone is not one of the things making it harder."

Part of the work we do at our Center for Racial Reconciliation is workshops, and one of our most utilized activities is the privilege walk. It's a sociological experience where people stand in a line at the back of a room and questions are asked to the group at large. Depending on your answers to these questions, you might take a step forward or stay where you are. If you've never feared the police, step forward. If your parents can afford to give you a down payment on your home, step forward. If you've never had to be on financial aid at school, step forward. If your parents graduated from college, step forward, and so on. These questions are designed to note the social challenges people of color have experienced, and the opportunities white siblings have received. The end result is usually clear: Once the walk is over, most of the minorities are in the back, and the people in the front or toward the front are white. In short, this exercise helps people who don't believe in or like the idea of white privilege see that whiteness is indeed the standard and, if they are white, it shows them what privileges have been afforded to them according to that standard. They see that that standard is where they live even if they've never recognized it before.

I remember one year there was this white man who did the privilege walk with us and, let me tell you, this guy was eager. He just knew the exercise wouldn't "work" on him. He told me he'd seen it before, and he knew it wasn't going to get him because his life had been difficult in every possible way.

Well, we did the walk and at the end, this man found himself midway to the front of the room and he was devastated.

When the workshop was over, he pulled me aside.

"How're you doing?" I asked him. He looked at me, distressed.

"Pastor," he said, "I grew up poor. I did not go to college. I don't have a formal education. We didn't have money or resources growing up. I was a poor, uneducated white man, Pastor, and I just knew I'd be at the back of the line... How is it that I found myself in front of college-educated Black women as a poor, uneducated white man?"

You see, at that moment he had come face-to-face with something I and many of my siblings of color have seen too often: His whiteness had extended him privileges his whole life that he'd been swimming in, so much so that he didn't see them, know them, or recognize them. He never feared the police. He might not have gone to college, but his parents did. He never had the color of his skin get in the way of living his life. These things are so subtle, though, that the privilege walk shows us what we already know: Privilege is really hard to see. Whiteness is hard to see. But when we step back and we're honest about the reality of the impact—not the intent, but the impact—of whiteness, we find ourselves unexpectedly complicit to this standard. Whether it's by us thinking less of ourselves as people of color or you thinking that your white skin hasn't had any impact on your life—we become complicit.

That man that day realized he had advantages he never even recognized before, and he walked away shocked at the truth of his reality.

White privilege can be so hard to see. It's not as obvious or overt as white supremacy. But we cannot deny that it's there.

WHO YOU CALLING A RACIST . . . ?

I'll never forget being in high school and going to basketball games. In the stands, the cheer section was always the cool, fun place to be because we made coming up with cheers and sayings and phrases an art. One of the big ones, though, we couldn't take credit for.

Stadiums and gyms across the country heard this cry go up when their home team was playing opponents with a great offensive advantage: "Defense! Defense! Defense!"

It's a simple trick: If you want to stop the opposition from coming, you have to have a strong defense to slow them down, trip them up, or stop them altogether. Well, this works great when shutting down a shot in basketball, but it also works great in shutting down conversations that could lead to transformation, vulnerability, honesty, and healing from some of the things that have held us captive in this country.

Now is not the time to yell, "Defense! Defense! Defense!" Honestly, I think the great aversion to this conversation alone is what makes it so hard to read these books and engage in these talks, because they conjure up our worst fears that we are somehow biased. That somehow prejudice has crept into our lives and gotten real comfy. That through privilege and dynamics we haven't seen before, we might somehow find ourselves having contributed to the problem all around. And these fears can all be gathered under one big fear: For many people, the worst thing that can happen is to be called a racist.

Yeah, that is scary. But I'd like to offer another perspective: We all bring bias and prejudice to the table. We are all from a place that comes with its own prejudices and assumptions, and we bring that along with us as we move through life.

Now, racism is when that prejudice is met with power, and it makes a system. That is the literal definition of "racism." We know the horror and damage of racism and how much destruction it brings. That said, our defenses spring up at the mere mention of racism because racism itself and the title of "racist" are things we don't want anywhere near us.

But I think there's something even worse than being a racist: being an unrepentant racist. Seeing all the assumptions and prejudices you've acquired in life and sticking with them unapologetically.

We have to understand that Satan's strategy is to get us to think that racism doesn't exist. He wants to convince us it isn't real. I've never seen so much incentive for people to think and feel that racism is not real—it's from a long time ago, that stuff doesn't happen anymore, there isn't really a problem, someone has friends of color, so they can't be a racist. I'll add that I personally think that most of the time, people don't intend to be racist. A lot of time prejudice and microaggressions stem from ignorance. But to think that all people don't intend to be racist? That's just unrealistic. Whiteness, white supremacy, white privilege—it all has an agenda to push defense and end the game and any opportunity for freedom, wholeness, peace, or deliverance.

I've seen it all over the place the last few years: People are so defensive of the label, system, and institution of racism that they step all over people's mourning. When a Black or brown person is gunned down, before the body is even cold, people are already looking for reasons why the victim "deserved" what they got, as if "not being a saint" is grounds enough to be gunned down at a traffic stop, in the street, or in one's own home. People have developed an inability to sit and to love beyond their ideology and fixed position of understanding because the fear of the label is so great.

Satan's strategy is to convince us that racism isn't real—that it's just some part of the liberal leftist agenda. It's hard for the Holy Spirit to convict us of something that we don't believe is real.

The Holy Spirit wants to open our hearts and eyes to see privilege, to see internalized racial oppression within ourselves. Now is not the time to keep our eyes closed—it is not the time to go blind and believe Satan's lies. Now is the time to let our eyes be opened to God's kingdom agenda.

I WAS ROBBED

In 2005, I had the opportunity to go to South Africa with my mentor and dear friend Bryan Loritts. He would be preaching there. We initially went to Johannesburg and then made our way to Soweto, where Bryan was scheduled to preach at a community church. Let me just say it was amazing. This church was like a big gymnasium: high ceilings, rows and rows of folding chairs, and a big stage where my friend would soon be preaching the word of God. As we checked out the space I kept taking in a single thought: "I am in the Motherland!" This was my first time ever in Africa, a dream destination for someone whose ancestors were stolen from there. Just to be on the soil of the home of my ancestors was so humbling and so wonderful and overwhelming to take in.

So, as the service started, I knew I was in for an experience—and it was just that. In fact, it was and remains one of the most profound experiences of my whole life. I mean, the music alone was enough to bring me to tears. The harmonies were flowing around the room like wind, the choir and the congregation sang with one voice so that you could hear singing and praise to the Lord all around, 360 degrees. The voices and tones and rhythms and harmonies were unlike anything I had ever heard before. The spirit in the room honestly felt supernatural—and that's because it was! The Holy Spirit was with us in that space, and it was powerful.

Then, it happened. These older women in their seventies, eighties, nineties, along with the little kids following—they started dancing in the aisles. They were moving from side to side, dancing with reckless abandon in a full display of joy and exuberance. They started what I can only describe from my American perspective as a soul train line, and they started pulling people from the crowd to dance with them, snatching people from their seats and adding them to the celebration. In moments they grabbed me, and I was thrown into the dance. I was just twentysomething years old, dancing in Africa in a church on Sunday morning, and people were shouting and clapping and celebrating and crying, and it hit me: This was what I was robbed of that day at the choir competition. This was what Ricky and I were on the threshold of when we sat down.

I realized that this—dancing and raising my voice—is who I am. That this was natural to me. That this was how I am meant to express joy! I finally recognized that the quiet, stoic victory at the choir competition was only so because it was a white standard. Whereas for me? For my people? A display of joy is natural and welcome. The ancestors made that clear; the students of Piney Woods carried that legacy in that moment of celebration. I realized that in the time between the choir competition and the South Africa church service, I'd been given a vision of whiteness, and I lost myself, causing me to live in shade and not shine.

We are an emotive people. We are a dancing people, a celebratory people. We are a moving and grooving people—we display our joy with our bodies. It still shocks me that I found myself in a city I'd never been before, in a church I'd never attended before, around these people I'd never seen before, and in the midst of all that, I'd never felt more at home before. This dancing and celebration is in my bones. These are my people and our expression—this is how we respond. In that moment of joy, I also found myself mourning and reflecting on all the things whiteness had robbed me of in this life, and it showed me that the most dangerous thing about whiteness, and why we need to come against it so strongly regardless of our color or ethnicity, is that it robs God's children of the Imago Dei of our identity. It robs us of how we are made—the diversity of His creation! We, too, are made in His image.

I'm reminded of Paul in Ephesians as he stands back and looks at us, all of us, as we are: this poiema, this masterpiece—God's masterpiece. In that moment I was reminded that I am made in God's image just as I am. My people tell the story of God the same as our white siblings, and we are a masterpiece made in His image. I am fearfully and wonderfully made! So why am I trying to fit into whiteness when God has made me beautifully and intentionally and masterfully in my Blackness?

My God. It struck me that I had been hoodwinked, bamboozled, led astray, run amok![1]

Whiteness has been trying my whole life to rob me of who I was created to be. It has been trying to rob me of my heritage, my voice, my genetic makeup, all so that I could be something else that, in truth, I could never really be. For no other reason than this long-lasting attempted theft, we must cast down whiteness so it can't stop us from trying to be what God intended us to be.

Friends, Revelation 7:9 has become an anchor text for me:

> After this I looked, and there before me was a great multitude that no one could count, from every nation, tribe, people and language, standing before the throne and before the Lamb. They were wearing white robes and were holding palm branches in their hands.

Scripture says it right out: My nation, tribe, tongue, and race matter to Jesus Christ. Race and ethnicity won't be suddenly done away with when we all get to the throne. This verse calls out the bad theology that Jesus washes us and makes us all the same in His blood. It is wrong and, frankly, not even biblical, to say that race doesn't matter. God calls us to oneness, but not sameness. We will all be with Him together—every race, tribe, nation, and tongue.

I fear that many of us have adopted this idea that when we get to heaven, it will be all sectioned off. There will be a white section, a Black section, an Asian section, a Latino section (though if I can get real real quick, you all know the Black section would have great music; I mean, we know it'd be off the chain—but I digress). But this isn't the truth. No, the picture of heaven is that we will all be there together declaring as one voice, "Worthy is the Lamb who was slain!"

So, I caution you to get rid of this "solution" of colorblindness. I remember hearing one white woman's argument for not seeing color: She said that it was because Martin Luther King Jr. himself stated he had a dream that his children would not be judged by the color of their skin, but by the content of their character. So, in her head, she heard that we were told to not pay any attention to color, and only to content. But friends, she missed it. That was not what Dr. King was saying at all. To ignore color is to rob me. Dr. King's words were a call not to judge, not an invitation to ignore. We love our siblings by seeing them, all of them.

See me and all that God created me to be. Love me for what God has made. Love me, don't rob me.

LET'S PLAY MONOPOLY

I remember a sermon by a good friend of mine, Pastor Ben Parkinson. Ben's a white pastor down in southern Tennessee and he talks about the impact of whiteness and white privilege like this:

Albert, let's say we're going to play a game of Monopoly, but before we play, two generations before us will play. Our grandfathers will play, then our fathers, and then you and I. Three generations of white men and Black men. We're going to play generational Monopoly.

So, our grandfathers sit down and play, and as is the general rule of Monopoly, once you pass Go, you collect $200. Now, when our grandfathers play and go to collect their $200, my white grandfather punches your Black grandfather in the mouth and takes his money. Every single time they pass Go; this happens. So, they play like that for a whole generation.

Next our fathers play. This time my white father tells your Black father, Albert, "I don't know why my dad punched your dad in the mouth and took his $200. That was totally inappropriate and wrong and we're not going to play like that anymore. So, every time we pass Go, you can go ahead and collect your $200 and I will not violently abuse you. However—you cannot own Park Place or the railways or put any homes or hotels on your property."

And so, our fathers play this way for a whole generation.

Finally, it's our turn. I say to you, Albert, that my white father played your Black father for a whole generation allowing him to get his money, but to not play the most influential part of the game. Well, now it's our time. I don't know why my white grandfather did what he did or why my white father did what he did, but I want you to know as we're about to sit down and play: I won't take your money or bodily abuse you, and you can buy whatever property you want to buy.

So, then Ben stretches out his hand to shake mine and says, "Okay, Albert, are we all even now? We're all even, right? We're equal and we're playing with the same rules, so it's all okay."

But we have to ask ourselves, are we equal? Is it okay? In that scenario, Ben's family has three generations of privilege and advantage. And mine? What is the impact of three generations of disadvantage and unfairness? Ben and I may sit down to play and finally be equal, but what has happened is not equitable.

See, there's a difference between equality and equity. As we dig into this conversation about the impact of whiteness and white privilege, we have to have an honest talk about the differences between equality and equity. We have to recognize that generations have gone before us, and it has significantly impacted where people of color, especially Black people, are today.

Redlining and community pacts, a banking system that refused Black people loans so they couldn't build wealth or equity—there are systems still in place today that have been in play for generations, that are still shaping institutions and the livelihoods of Blacks and people of color. So, I ask you, how can we come to the cross and say because Black people can get loans and move into white neighborhoods that it's "all equal now"? How can we make the claim that we love the Lord and that everything is better now because it's not overtly the way it was?

Friends, we can't. Jesus is interested in equality and equity. He's come to restore all things. Everything Satan has come to steal, kill, and destroy, Christ has come to bring life and life more abundant. So, when we come into this conversation, we cannot say "It's all good now" and move forward. We have to look at what has been stolen and pursue both equity and equality because Jesus has come to make it all right, from start to finish.

In Scripture we can turn to the story of Zacchaeus. If you grew up in the church, you're probably familiar with it, but here's the truncated version: Zacchaeus was a tax collector, that is, someone who actively took advantage of and stole from the people in his community by raising and collecting taxes. As a result, he lived a pretty cushy life at the expense of his neighbors. Needless to say, Zacchaeus was not a popular guy. Well, one day Jesus was coming through town and Zacchaeus wanted to see Him. Because he was short, he couldn't see over the crowd, so he climbed a sycamore tree to see the Lord. Well, here's the twist: Just as Zacchaeus was looking to see Jesus, Jesus was looking to see him. Jesus saw him in the tree and called him down, told him He was coming to his home to eat.

In those times and in that culture, going to someone's home was like an affirmation. To have someone come to your home and share a meal was one of the most generous and open invites you could give them. So, when Jesus says this, He's choosing Zacchaeus in full display of everyone. The text wants us to understand that Zacchaeus—being who he is and what he is—is the least likely person to be chosen by Jesus for anything. But because Jesus sees him and calls out to him, Zacchaeus is changed in his heart. He immediately comes down from the tree and tells Jesus that before He can come to his home, he, Zacchaeus, must confess that he has taken advantage of people and perpetuated an unjust system. He says that before he can go further into a relationship with Jesus, he has to acknowledge his wrongs and now make them right. He has to give back what he's taken and restore what he's ruined. In other words, he has to disadvantage himself so that he may advantage others—just as Jesus does.

As Jesus saw Zacchaeus, He also sees you and me. He invites us to come and journey with Him in this intimate relationship, and it is such a radical invite because we don't deserve it! Like Zacchaeus we are sinful, and we don't deserve to be at Jesus' table—but He invites us anyway. And in response to His invitation, we must show love that disadvantages self so that we may advantage others. This is the impact of Christ's love.

We don't respond to whiteness and white privilege this way for political correctness or popularity. We don't do it because it's become a trend. We do it because it's what Jesus has done for us, and because it is what we should do for one another: make things right and do what we can to bring heaven on earth. We must have a heart transformed by Christ and pursue rightness, not whiteness. We must right what has been wrong for a very long time.

MORE THAN "NOT A RACIST"

We talked about the great fear around the label of "racist" a little while ago, but I want us to go deeper. I'll never forget being in a staff meeting with a sister church where the staff wanted to talk about whiteness and racism. Their end goal was this: to not be racist. This was a mostly white staff and, honestly, they mainly wanted to get enough information and experience so they could confidently say they were not a racist place with racist people.

I fear that this has become the goal for so many, and I have to be honest in saying that it is not enough. God is calling us to so much more than just not being racist.

I remember during that meeting getting an interesting question. I can't recall the question itself, but it was in the spirit of "C'mon, haven't we gotten better? Isn't racism over? Things are clearly better, right?"

In response, I told them the story of the abusive father.

There was a father with two sons and, for whatever reason, he would come into his younger son's room each night and abuse him. One day, in what seemed to be a moment of courage, the older son came to his younger brother and told him, "Hey, I know what Dad is doing at night. I've heard him and seen him, and I know. I want you to know I see you and I'm praying for you."

Well, the younger son looked at his older brother with tears in his eyes and said, "If you know Dad's doing this, it's not enough to see me and pray." He told his brother that he needed him to stand with him and fight their dad off, that he needed his sibling to make a difference with him, not just acknowledge the abuse and pray it away. "I need you to stand with me and fight," he said.

As a Black man, this is my invitation to my white siblings: It's not enough to see what whiteness is or to know the impact of it. As siblings, you have to know and understand that whiteness, white supremacy, and white privilege have abused your siblings of color for generations, and it was never okay. I am not just inviting you but pleading with you to not only pray and see, but to stand up and fight this with us. We must put whiteness and its two brothers, supremacy and privilege, to death, and we have to do it together in Jesus' name.

CHAPTER 5

DEAR BEREAVED

REQUIEM: A TIME TO MOURN

One of my fondest memories from my childhood is the weekly family time we would spend gathered around my parents' bed. It would be me, my sisters, Mom, and Dad. We would be gathered around their king-size bed, elbows to mattress, chins in hands, and heads bowed in prayer. We did this most Sundays, and one by one each of us would say a prayer during that time, but Mom's was always the longest.

She would have a laundry list of prayers that she would go through each time. It would stretch on and on, but she was always sure to end it with these words: "... and God, please bless the bereaved family."

Every single week the bereaved family made the list, and as a young boy I began to think that "bereaved" was a last name. Each week there were friends who didn't make Mom's list, family members who didn't make her list, church members who didn't make her list, but you could bet that the Bereaved family would be on there, and they always were. I soon started to think that the poor Bereaved family was just really unfortunate; they were always going through some really hard stuff because Mom always prayed for them no matter what. Well, I soon discovered that "bereaved" was not in fact a last name, but a term for any family mourning the death of a loved one.

I learned that the bereaved were those who had loved ones pass away and were now left with great holes in their hearts for their family members. They were those who had been left behind, who had lost someone or many someones and were struggling with that absence. My mother knew that such families needed long, consistent prayer because they were suffering such a great loss—and so she prayed every Sunday without fail.

When I was in college, I was part of the choir, and I'll never forget singing the spirituals, gospels, and classical pieces that our director, Dr. Bobby G. Cooper, assigned. He had a knack for finding some of the most beautiful music I had ever heard. One day, Dr. Cooper, who soon became one of my longtime mentors, introduced our choir to a piece of music unlike anything we had ever sung before. It took a long time to learn it and it was more challenging than we were used to. It was called "Requiem." We learned that this piece was often used for Catholic Masses for the dead.

That first time I heard "Requiem," I was taken with the melody, the tones, and the lyrics stretched over several long and sorrowful bars. This music was long and dark. It's what my son Isaac would call "emotional" or "sad" music. As the harmonies came together you couldn't help but just feel sad. But it was a beautiful sad—it created a beautiful place to sit while sad. I think it captured the essence of unexpected death and sudden sorrow, and ultimately it reminded me of one of the first times I remember losing someone close to me: my grandfather, Reverend Tate.

In Mississippi, the day of the funeral, cars and limousines come to the home of the bereaved to collect the family, and they drive to the church. There they have an amazing celebration service for the life that's been lost, then they get back into the cars to head to the gravesite. When I lost my grandfather, it was the first time ever in my life riding in a limousine or seeing a police escort. There were motorcycles, and then the hearse, then the limos, and then all the people who had been at the funeral. There were hundreds. I tell you, it was a sea of cars—a line that stretched as far back as you could see, headed toward the freeway. Such was Reverend Tate's legacy that an exceedingly large crowd came to his homegoing. He had touched so many lives and pastored so many people that when it was his time to go on, many came to pay their respects. As we were all driving in this great procession, I remember looking out the window and noticing something: As we rode, other cars were pulling over, slowing down, stopping completely, and letting us pass. People who weren't even connected to or affected by the funeral were getting out of the way to let us go as the police officers and the hearse went by. I remember tears began welling up in my eyes as I saw this—people were stopping to honor my grandad and our family. People who didn't even know us. All they knew was that the hearse meant someone had passed, and so the people in the cars following it, the family and friends, were sad, devastated, and changed by the reality of death. While these people on the road couldn't actually do anything for us, they did what they could: pulled over and stopped to honor Grandad and make space for our grief as we made the journey to the gravesite.

I believe that devastation and death can be matched only by honor and respect, and these cars on the road did just that. Their mere actions were like the melodies and bars of the "Requiem"—they created and maintained a space to sit and be sad.

Mom prayed for the bereaved family because they needed all the honor, support, and space they could get. And in this life, everyone gets their turn to be part of the bereaved.

I have a friend who suffered a devastating loss. She suddenly lost her husband, a man who was only in his thirties. He just dropped dead. About six weeks after his death, I got up on a Saturday morning, grabbed some breakfast burritos and coffee, and sat down with my friend and some of her family to talk. She told me about the day her husband died and just how this time of mourning hit her: One day they had a regular family, and the next she was in mourning.

This friend has an iPhone and uses facial recognition to unlock her screen. She told me that in that onset of grief and mourning, she cried so hard and so much that she couldn't open her phone. Her face had been so changed by grief—her eyes so filled with tears, her face so contorted with sadness—that her phone literally did not recognize her. You see, the mourning had begun and taken hold. She had been utterly changed.

What's so significant to me about this is that there's something so natural and human about mourning and creating space for grief. These spaces should and often do come naturally when someone you thought would be here is suddenly gone.

On May 25, 2020, when George Floyd was murdered, there was a young girl who, honestly, changed the trajectory of how this particular Black death would affect the nation and the world. Her name is Darnella Frazier. As that police officer held his knee in George Floyd's neck for those nine minutes and twenty-nine seconds, she pulled out her phone and recorded everything.

There was now a family out there whose loved one's death was captured on video, and of course, the video went viral worldwide. Everyone with an internet connection could see this man die because a police officer brutally put a knee in his neck. We saw him die. We saw his tears, his last words, his life literally leaving him.

About a week later, on the day of George's funeral, I still hadn't seen the video. I refused to watch it. It's just such a strange, unnatural, and wrong thing to see someone murdered in broad daylight, let alone to see it pop up on your screen as you're scrolling through social media. It should really mess with our heads how easily the public was given access to a video portraying a man's murder. We should not be desensitized to it; we should not be comfortable seeing something like that anywhere. So, I didn't watch it. I avoided it as best I could because I knew I couldn't handle it.

But on the day of the funeral, as the cars were pulling up to the bereaved family's home and the escort was there to lead the way, not only were the cars stopping—the world had also stopped.

On that day, I watched the video.

I watched this man's murder as his family prepared for his funeral. When I finished the video, I couldn't help thinking about myself as a Black man who has had his own encounters with police, and that connection brought me to tears. I was grieving as if I were part of the Floyd family, as if I were physically at his funeral. In all honesty, it felt like a national funeral because we had all seen a murder and we all felt the grief and pain. Just as the video finished on my screen, another video immediately started playing. With a sound like nails on a chalkboard, I heard a piercing change in tone. It was the antithesis of grief, mourning, or even compassion. I remember being caught by the title—something to the effect of "I Will Not Make You A Martyr."

Before I could even adjust my screen, a young, Black conservative woman started talking about George Floyd. I was immediately drawn in. This young woman was passionate, she was articulate, she had a definite way with words. As I'm listening, her words become more and more like a screech in my ears. She was talking about George Floyd, but she was mainly talking about his criminal record.

She spoke about her understanding of his failures and flaws and mistakes and the criminal acts of his past, and she declared that she would not make him a martyr, nor would she celebrate his life. As she went on, I began to hear what was to me some of the most unkind, venomous, visceral, and godless speech I could ever imagine or remember hearing in my life. It felt like the complete opposite of empathy, love, and grace. Friends, I was so grieved to hear these words spilling from the mouth of a young Black woman who seemed to be convinced that George Floyd was not worthy of sorrow—that he wasn't worthy of prayer, and neither was his family; he wasn't even worth pulling over on the side of the road for. To be clear, she didn't say these words, but her disdain and this sentiment was evident to me in her tone.

To me, this woman seemed to make it clear that she was certain the dark tones and elongated melodies of the "Requiem" were not appropriate for George Floyd and his family. They did not deserve a beautiful place for their grief. Maybe, just maybe, she was unaware that the Floyd family's faces had changed because of their deep mourning—or maybe she didn't care. Why would she choose this moment, the day of his funeral, to talk about his lack of worth? Why did she choose today to suggest he was not made in the image of God, and so was not worthy of grace? Every image she presented of him seemed to be marked with his flaws, and she emphatically exclaimed to never celebrate his life or make him anything more than the worst thing he's ever done.

Parenthetically, I want to point out that no one was trying to make George Floyd a martyr. No one was trying to celebrate his crimes or his flaws, let alone erase them. This man had been killed for no reason, but that doesn't make him a martyr. Across the world we were mourning the fact that he was killed, that his life was taken brutally and disgustingly, and that we all had the unfortunate vantage point of seeing his killing happen in real time. We were there to grieve, but this young woman seemed to be there for something else.

It seemed to me that her words and her hate were so bitter, so self-righteous, that listening to her literally felt evil. It was so foreign to my soul to hear a person speak this way, and it honestly felt demonic. I guess what I'm trying to say is it felt extreme because it was; it felt so evil because it was completely absent of compassion.

MUG SHOT JESUS

As I listened to these words about George Floyd, it struck me that she was speaking as if who he was disqualified him from being honored in death. As if, somehow, the worst thing you've ever done immediately disqualifies you and your family from receiving compassion and empathy in the moment of your death.

Now, I'm not sure if this woman proclaims to be a Christian, but I do know that plenty of Christians certainly proclaim her perspective. The funny thing is, I think that if we were somehow able to walk into the attorney general's office in Rome, and if there were some way to look through their official court records, and if they'd had the technology at that time, I'm sure we would find a mug shot of Jesus. We have to remember that leading up to His crucifixion, Jesus went to trial, and the verdict came back guilty. The people shouted, "Crucify Him! Crucify Him! Crucify Him!" It would serve us all to know and to remember that Jesus died with a criminal record.

Honestly, I could do several chapters on criminals and how we view them in our society, but despite who the criminal is or what they've done, we must be clear that the blood of Jesus Christ cleanses and expunges all records of our past. Simply put, we are not the worst thing we've ever done.

With cancel culture, often what we do is something my dear friend and fellow pastor Bryan Loritts calls "taking a snapshot." When we do this, we essentially take a picture of someone at their worst and then make that their personal and permanent profile picture. So, if someone were to Google you, there would be your worst moment on full display, and it would be the only image of you that mattered anymore. But Jesus doesn't work like that. With Jesus, our life is not a picture, it's more of a movie. If you get stuck on one bad scene, then you risk missing the redemptive work Christ is doing in that life. In reality, the film keeps rolling and God keeps working and redemption keeps coming—His grace never runs out. We cannot treat people like they are their worst moments. We cannot treat ourselves that way. Failures are not fatal—my failure doesn't take me out of the game, and it doesn't make me unworthy of the Imago Dei, and neither do yours. Failure is not meant to steal compassion from a life and from a family. The very nature of God is that He's doing a redemptive work and it is lifelong.

So, watching this video of this woman detailing Floyd's criminal record is not what Jesus would do. Honestly, Jesus would probably pull out His own mug shot and show it to remind us how the Roman soldiers saw Him. But, friends, we have to remember that three days later the world would see Him as a reigning king! Don't hold people to their mug shots. Don't hold Jesus to His and don't hold me to mine. I won't hold you to yours. None of us should hold this young lady to hers.

I want to be clear that I have no problem being honest about George Floyd's life. He was not a martyr, nor was he a saint or a savior. But he was loved by the savior, and for that reason alone he deserved better. My hope is to treat everyone with the love and respect they deserve simply because they are made in God's image despite their record or their words or their beliefs.

SPEARED BY SIBLINGS

Over the late spring and summer of 2020, my DMs were abnormally full. I had hordes of messages from well-meaning white siblings asking me if I'd heard this one Black person speak, and what I thought of her. Had I seen her video? Had I heard this one Black person that made my white sibling feel comfortable and validated in their bias and their perspective? She confirmed all the same perspectives they held, and she was Black! Had I heard of her?

To answer that question, I'm reminded of something my friend Jamie Sutton often says: Be leery of Black people who white people love and who few Black people follow.

This woman holds and espouses a very conservative, vitriolic view, and it honestly breaks my heart that so many of my white siblings thought to send her video to me. The message behind the action was clear: You're Black and she's Black, so you must agree with her! To that I say, gently: Black people are not and never have been a monolith.

When you paint the picture of what love is and what the fruits of the Spirit are, you don't see any of those present in the video. It lacks kindness, empathy, integrity, and also truth—so why were Christian siblings celebrating it and passing it around? Her vitriol went viral, and it was being sent to me, to other pastors, to family members, as if her viewpoint was worth propping up. And it all makes me wonder: What's the motive? This is a funeral, and her message is "Don't love this guy! Don't mourn for him! Don't make him a martyr and don't use him to raise a greater conversation about race and police brutality! He does not deserve it..."

I just have to say that anything that makes you feel better about loving your neighbor less is probably godless. It is a missed opportunity to be like Christ, and rather than starting a conversation fueled by hate, we should have been trying to figure out how to give more love and be there for the bereaved family—and in this instance, the bereaved family was the Black community and much of America, and most of the world at large.

It's like no one pulled over that day. It's like people actively drove into the procession to disrupt it and ruin it. These actions were disrespectful and clearly say that George Floyd was not worthy. The way I see it, these moments when we have the opportunity to love and instead hurt people? We are spearing them. I call this being speared by our siblings. When white siblings show up with questions, when they share videos with messages like that, it's honestly so painful to see and experience. Instead of embracing one another and spreading love, too often we stab one another with indifference and defensiveness or just total denial of the reality of someone's pain. I've said it before, and I'll repeat now: We shouldn't have to defend our tears.

CRISIS IN THE COMMENTS

Unfortunately, our world has come down to conversations that exist in 280 characters on Twitter or the comments sections of Facebook and Instagram. We go toe-to-toe in the DMs and hold little regard for the person behind the screen. Especially in this season where so much has been happening, there quickly came a crisis in the comments with people clashing and fighting over everything from the pandemic to police brutality to whether or not Asian hate was really happening. Enemies have been cultivated in the comments and hearts have been broken. But I want to point something out: Christ is drawn to the brokenhearted. People of color are brokenhearted, and God is drawn to the brokenhearted. Scripture says blessed are those who mourn for they will be comforted. And I think that comfort comes from Him—but also from His children, our siblings.

In March 2021 when the Atlanta spa shootings took place, in which nearly all the victims were Asian, I posted something on behalf of my Asian siblings to let them know their pain was my pain, that it was felt, seen, and validated. This shooting was just another instance in a long string of anti-Asian hate crimes and behaviors that had been spiking since the onset of the pandemic, in which our Asian siblings were attacked in the streets, harassed, verbally abused, and now shot and killed. Well, a white sibling left a comment on my post that said, "I appreciate your post, but where's the evidence this was Asian hate?"

When I saw that, I couldn't help but think about how, once again, we were at a funeral. It was not the conversation we should have been having just then. While we were trying to honor the bereaved family and show compassion for their experience, this man was demanding evidence of it.

There was another post where a crisis came to the comments. Another Black body had been killed unjustly and the community was mourning. We were again at a funeral needing love, and there was someone in the comments demanding logic and arguing the facts of the incident and sequence of events as if to figure out whether or not this Black body deserved it. I honestly wanted to scream at the top of my lungs, "WE ARE AT A FUNERAL." But it often feels like no one is listening, or that few will care even if they hear me.

These moments of tragedy are opportunities to show up with love, not logic, to see others' experiences and not demand evidence or be drilled by the heartless. How we love in these moments is so significant. We have to ask ourselves: How would Jesus show up in this thread? What comments would Jesus make in this post about pain and burden?

Before you make a comment or send a message, maybe you should go back to those old-school bracelets everyone used to wear and ask yourself, "What would Jesus do?"

Because Jesus is drawn to the brokenhearted and He comforts them. As His children and as siblings, we are to do the same.

RAISING CONCERNS AND REFUSING COMPASSION

Often, the pain and frustration caused by my white siblings comes in these arguments and flash points when we're stepping to the table to have a hard conversation about race, and they raise concerns but refuse to show any compassion. These incidents, these murders, these moments of brutality and racism, seem to trigger some of my white siblings and expose their intent. They ask questions like, "But what about Black-on-Black crime?" when statistically[1] it is clear that people murder people in their own communities everywhere. More white people kill white people, more Asian people kill Asian people, more Latino people kill Latino people, and on and on. So, logically, we can turn the question around and ask, "What about white-on-white crime?" When my white siblings ask that question, they make it sound like violence is something Black people do, and not something humans do. And that is just not true.

They ask, "What about all the violence in Chicago? If you hate violence and brutality, why aren't you mad about that?" But what we need to understand is that when this question is being asked, they only ask it after a Black body has been killed or abused. I think the better question is "Why are you asking that right now?"

See, what these white siblings don't understand about Chicago is that there are thousands of pastors and faith leaders working to make it a better place. I personally know dozens of pastors who are working

hard every day on the streets to build a better city. There are min-
istries and programs and people working to make a positive impact
in the area. Black religious leaders in Chicago love their home; they
love their city and they're fighting for it. But if we're going to be honest, the white siblings who ask the question really don't care about
that. All they care about is making the point and deflecting away
from the issues of racial injustice and systemic racism. So, I'd like to
ask these siblings: "Where are your receipts? What have you done
in and for Chicago? Show me your prayer journal—have you prayed
about it? Have you gone to help? Have you made an impact?" But I
already know what the answer is. Because these siblings don't actually
care beyond their argument. The question isn't coming from a place
of concern and compassion; it's coming from a disingenuous place.
They desire to discredit real issues so that they can stay comfortably in
their seats and in their bias that says it's just a Black people problem,
not a family problem—and definitely not a white people problem.

In the midst of all these Black deaths and the protests that broke
out across the world in the summer of 2020, soon some riots broke
out as well. By and large, the protests were positive, peaceful, and safe
where no one was harmed. But there were for sure some that turned
violent, and some buildings were destroyed. I know of many pastors
who took to their pulpits in those days preaching against riots, protests,
and the organizations that supported the protestors. They said that as
Christians, we should follow the law and not break it by protesting.

Well, also at that time the government was wrestling with which
businesses and buildings could be open and which could not under
pandemic restrictions. Churches, considering their communal nature,
run the risk of becoming superspreader events, so they were not allowed
to open. And so, as this rule rolled over the country, white pastors
ran to the internet to declare their frustration and anger about this

"injustice." They began declaring that they should have the right to open, that they were essential, and that they would refuse to wear masks and distance to boot. Petitions were passed around and protests were held. They were willing to break whatever law was in place for the sake of their cause. I remember seeing all of this and thinking, "Oh wow, so you do know how to protest. So, you do have passion and a fierce resolve to not let something you disagree with go down on your watch." But not too long before these same pastors were preaching against demonstrations and protests, all while ignoring the issues that provoked the demonstrations and protests to begin with.

It was all such a juxtaposition—they were more upset about broken glass in a building than a dead, broken body in the street. These pastors, these Christians, were more passionate about vandalized property than they were about victimized people. Oh, how you love your buildings, but what about our bodies? It struck me that these siblings for sure know how to protest, just not for us. These white siblings continued to raise their concerns about our protests, but they refused to display compassion for our pain—and that feels like spears in our sides from our siblings.

INVITATION TO LOVE

I'm sure there have been fights at funerals before, but I think we can all agree that brawling at the gravesite is not a good idea. These flash points in our culture and moments of crisis in our country demand the best of us, but I keep seeing the worst of us. These tragedies are not a time to fight, they're a time to show up with as much spiritual fruit and love as we possibly can. These moments are when we must showcase our love, light, and salt that comes directly from our relationship with Jesus Christ. What would it mean if more of us showed the world Christ in the comments?

I want to end by saying I get it. One of the problems and great losses in our modern world is nuance. Everything is so divided now that there's little understanding between us. These conversations are hard, and they cannot be had in the comments. We need more words, not fewer. We need more conversations and safe places to disagree and dialogue. The truth is that we are all biased and we need safe spaces at the family table to see and hear one another all while loving one another and expressing kindness, empathy, and care. If we do that, I think we will see and love and learn about our siblings. We can stop fighting each other and instead fight for one another and against the things that seek to oppress and deny us all.

These are undoubtedly complicated and challenging times and issues that are worthy of robust debate. It's not that we don't want to talk about these things—about logic and evidence and perspective. But just not at the funeral.

Rest in peace to all those who've been taken too soon. May we always keep the bereaved family in our prayers.

....

CHAPTER 6

DEAR ANCESTORS

SANKOFA

One of the reasons I decided to leave Mississippi and come out to Southern California was to attend Fuller Seminary. While I was there, I had a truly amazing time and was fully stretched and challenged in my studies and in the word.

My favorite professor at Fuller was Dr. Ralph Watkins, a dynamic Black man from the South who was a brilliant theologian, an author, and a passionate academic. Also, he would moonlight as a DJ.

In his classes we focused on his writing about theology and hip hop, the Black church, and how these two topics would intersect and interact in modern culture. We listened to Biggie and Tupac and put them in interaction and conversation with the church to see the theological influences on the music and lyrics, and it was just fascinating. His passion and energy in the classroom were absolutely unmatched, and you could just tell that he absolutely loved what he did. He was so enthusiastic that he made me want to study and learn more, which at that time in my life was really saying something. In short, his work was the epitome of innovation in my eyes, and I learned so much from him and the spaces he created.

One of my favorite classes with Dr. Watkins was one where we studied Thomas C. Oden's book *How Africa Shaped the Christian Mind*. At the start of the very first class of the course, Dr. Watkins told us that he was going to take us back in time and introduce us to the symbol and the idea of Sankofa.

"Sankofa" is a word in the Akan, Fante, and Twi languages of Ghana, and it literally translates "to retrieve" or "to go back and get." It breaks down like this:

San = To Return
Ko = To Go
Fa = To Fetch, Seek, and Take

It also refers to the Bono Adinkra symbol, which depicts a bird with its head turned backwards and its feet facing forward while it holds an egg in its beak. The concept of Sankofa is linked to the African proverb "Se wo were fi na wosankofa a yenkyi,"[1] which translates to "It is not wrong to go back and get that which you have forgotten." There is also a song of Sankofa, and it sounds like an island song. The melodies and lyrics really made me feel like I was flying backward in time, being transported to Africa—and Dr. Watkins played this song every single week as class got started.

So, with Dr. Watkins as our guide we went back and got what we'd forgotten of our heritage, our people, and the story of Africa and how it shaped Christianity and the Christian mind. Each week we would discover golden nuggets of wisdom and understanding of what Africa was and who the African people were—their intelligence, their power, their sacrifice. After every class I would leave feeling as though I'd recovered something I didn't have before, or perhaps something I'd forgotten that I once had a long time ago. I got to go back and get it.

One of the assignments in this particular class was to watch Alex Haley's *Roots*, the iconic miniseries based on his novel of the same name. Now, *Roots* originally aired in 1977, the very same year I was born. By the time I encountered it in college, it was so well-known and respected that it would come on television frequently and just be a whole event. So, my first exposure to Roots was as a respected classic, and as I watched this epic, I was immersed in not just the past, but my past.

For those who may not know, *Roots* is the story of author Alex Haley's family and his ancestor, Kunta Kinte (played by LeVar Burton), who was stolen from Africa and brought to the United States as a slave. Kinte and his descendants observe events throughout American history such as the Revolutionary War, slave uprisings, the Emancipation Proclamation, and more. Honestly, after watching *Roots* in seminary I realized it was something I should be watching every four to five years because the experience of watching it is itself Sankofa. There's so much that I didn't get before this, so much about my people, my history, and most of all the sacrifice that has been made for me to sit and write this today. Oh, what a cost has been paid.

One of the most significant scenes in *Roots* for me as a pastor, a church planter, and an ambassador for the multiethnic church is when Kinte tries to run away and is recaptured. There's an older slave on the same plantation named Fiddler (played by Lou Gossett Jr.) who tries to advocate for Kinte. So, he goes to the master's house and asks his missus if he can speak to the master. She's very sensitive about the master's time and lets Fiddler know it. "He's tending to the Scriptures," she tells him to make clear that whatever he has to say, he must keep it short. So, Fiddler walks in and on the master's desk is a table Bible—one of those huge, old Bibles—and the master is studying it beneath a magnifying glass. Now, in the shot, there's a window beyond the master, and through the window Fiddler and the audience can see Kunta Kinte hoisted up on the whipping post and hear his cries as he's about to be beaten for trying to run away. Cinematographically, the Bible sits between Fiddler and the master as Fiddler pleads with him to have mercy on Kinte. While Fiddler is talking, the master is engrossed in the big Bible. What I want us to notice here is that the master is studying Scripture closely while a great injustice is taking place in his own backyard. I want us to pay attention to how dangerous of a posture this is and how, unless we go back and get what we've missed, this posture is doomed to happen again and again.

See, we can get so preoccupied with the Scriptures in front of us that we miss what's going on behind and around us. For this reason alone, we have to pay attention to what we've forgotten. Sankofa is so necessary.

When I watch *Roots* and study this history, I can't help but think about the slave trade, the Jim Crow South, redlining, our school-to-prison pipeline—because these are all connected. As for all those who have gone before me—if they could see me now, sitting in my office in Southern California writing this book—I can't help but think about the price they paid so I can sit here and be who I am, where I am, and how I am. And certainly, we have a long way to go still, but oh, what a price has been paid! Lives have been lost, blood has been shed, fear and torture and abuse have been inflicted—and these sacrifices that they never chose to make overwhelm, shape, fuel, and drive me.

Thank you, ancestors. With tears in my eyes, thank you to all those who have gone before me and suffered at the hand of injustice. Many of you were not martyrs because you did not offer up your lives—they were taken. I'm grateful to you and I want to forever pause and think and go back.

I remember seeing a post on Instagram where a young Black woman was wearing a shirt that said, "I Am My Ancestors' Greatest Dreams." I just loved that when I saw it, and I pray that it may be so in my life.

YOUR BLOOD CRIES OUT

My good friend Rich Villodas is the lead pastor of New Life Fellowship Church out in Queens, in New York City. He's also the author of *The Deeply Formed Life,* and he's just one of the greatest writers and pastors I know. I love how he sits in passages, goes deep, and really teaches, and I love how he frames who the church is and who we're called to be. It's just such a beautiful thing, and I really learn so much from him. Well, once Rich and I were guests on a podcast together and while he was speaking, he said something that really resonated with me, especially when it comes to this message of love and racial reconciliation.

He noted that in the book of Genesis, there are two framing questions God asks humanity: the first to Adam and Eve, and the second to their son Cain. It's fundamental and noteworthy to notice that after Adam and Eve sin and hide, God asks them, "Where are you?"

I've found in my own research and life, and through conversations with Rich, that this is a question we all have to answer from God many times throughout our lives. We have to answer God about where we are, and we have to tell the truth about it. Without honest confession, there's no real change or healing that happens. So, where are you? Are you hiding? Are you sitting under shame and guilt and sin? Where are you?

In order to have transformation and accept the invitation of what God wants to do in our hearts and lives and our world, we must all first answer the question: Where are you?

The second fundamental question Rich points out that God asks comes after Adam and Eve's sons, Cain and Abel, have been born and grown up. As the story goes, Abel kept the flocks and Cain kept the soil. In time, Cain brought the fruit of the soil as an offering to the Lord, and Abel brought the choicest portions of the firstborn livestock as his offering. The Lord looked with favor on Abel and his offering, but not so with Cain. Because of this, Scripture says, Cain was angry and "his face was downcast." So, in Genesis 4:6–7 the Lord asks Cain, "Why are you angry? If you do what is right, will you not be accepted? But if you don't, sin crouches at your door ready to devour you, and you must master it."

Immediately after this, Cain asks Abel to come out into the field with him, and there in his fit of rage he murders his brother. Soon the Lord comes to Cain and asks him, "Where is your brother?" Cain responds by saying he doesn't know: "Am I my brother's keeper?" To this, the Lord says that yes, Cain is indeed his brother's keeper. And then the Lord tells Cain, "His blood cries out to me from the ground."

See, in order to really be in relationship with God, we have to answer these two fundamental questions: Where are you? Where is your brother?

Can't you see the two greatest commandments wrapped up in there? Love the Lord your God (where are you?) and love your neighbor as yourself (where is your brother?).

We have to be honest with God about where we are, which means we have to be committed to Him and open, not hiding in shame. And then we have to love our neighbors / our siblings. We are our brother's keeper, and our brother is our keeper. It matters that we know where our siblings are and how they are. On our journey of racial reconciliation, we cannot ignore these questions.

It's also important to note that God gives Cain a warning before he even does anything. The Lord sees the anger, frustration, and tension within Cain and takes note of it. He tells Cain that sin is crouching at the door ready to devour him, but he must rule over it. If he doesn't, sin will become all-consuming, and when sin grows up, it gives birth to death.

The book of Romans helps us here: In chapter 6, verse 23, Paul writes that "the wages of sin is death, but the gift of God is eternal life."

Sin crouches at each of our doors, and if we do not keep it in check and rule over it, it can devour us and lead to death. If we allow sin to grow up and mature, it looks like death, it becomes death, and it creates death.

The Lord asks Cain about his brother because it is indeed his responsibility to know where and how and who his brother is. The Lord then asks Cain: Can't he hear his brother's blood crying out from the ground? Can't he hear it? But the thing about sin is that as it matures and grows, it makes us able to ignore the blood on the ground. The injustice in the world, the plight of our siblings—we are soon unable to hear it or even see it because sin has grown up and taken us over.

As I look at world history and especially American history, there is so much blood on the ground. And it cries out. The blood of our ancestors cries out from the very ground we walk on, and we cannot keep moving as if it hasn't happened and as if we can't hear it. For believers in our pursuit of racial reconciliation, this is mandatory: We cannot live without acknowledging the past and the blood that cries out from the ground. And we cannot acknowledge the blood without

Sankofa, which reveals and helps us understand how we got here and why.

The blood on the ground has been ignored for too long, especially here in America, and we must hear it. To truly pursue racial reconciliation, we must go back and get what has been forgotten and omitted. If we are to pursue biblical racial reconciliation, we cannot give in to cancel culture and erase our past and what we've experienced. Currently, our culture is looking to completely cancel the conversation about race. There is policy and legislation being developed across the nation that would make it not only impossible but illegal to really talk about race in certain ways. Certain events won't be taught or spoken about in the classroom. Certain areas of study will be omitted from textbooks and conversations completely. This is a massive epidemic in our nation. The Trump administration recently halted funding to the department in our US government that's responsible for racial sensitivity training—training that would train and teach people to be sensitive to one another so that we might relate to and understand one another better. Because of this, this necessary training may no longer exist in public and government workplaces. So, we're experiencing not just cancel culture, but cancel policy that stops us from even having the conversation. But the reality remains that we cannot move forward and hope to reconcile what needs to be reconciled if we don't talk about it.

We have to go all the way back to the Garden to see what was broken then and what that has caused to be broken over the generations. We must go back to see these broken things so that we know what Jesus Christ is seeking to put back together through the gospel. Hint: It's all things! He wants to restore all things, all the way back to the first sin, all the way back to Cain and Abel and the blood on the ground.

In the name of Jesus Christ, we can't allow these cancel policies to stop us from going back and examining what has been hurt, stolen, abused, and wounded. I can't say it enough: If we can't even talk about these things, then we really aren't allowing for healing and redemption to begin.

My good friend Ben Cocherras is a pastor on the East Coast. When he had first moved out there, he took a bike ride around Washington, DC, to see the sights and the people and just get a little tour of his new home. While he was out, he came across this wall. As he cycled beside it, it got bigger and just expanded in height and length. Soon, Ben saw a little boy and his mother standing before the wall. The mother took the boy's finger and began tracing it along the wall where there are rows and rows of names engraved right into the granite; there was a tear in her eye. Farther along the wall, there was another family standing before the wall, pressing a piece of paper to the surface and shading over it with a pencil to capture a name. Yet another family was down the way placing flowers at the foot of the wall, and Ben saw they were holding hands and saying a prayer.

Well, Ben soon learned that this was none other than the Vietnam Veterans Memorial. The names on the wall belong to the men and women who gave their lives for the freedom of our nation. Their names were listed here to honor their sacrifice. They're listed so that the American people and the world would not forget what they've done. Each name there represented a person, a life, and a sacrifice— and it was there because it mattered. The blood that was shed matters, and through this memorial, their sacrifice still speaks.

I guess the point I'm trying to make is that if we really want to pursue racial justice and reconciliation, if we really want to right something that has been a terrible, bloody wrong in our history, we have to look at it and deal with it. We have to remember the people who have been hurt and lost. It's no secret that throughout American history this country has been in places that we aren't proud of (where are you?), but we still have to tell the truth about who we were then to understand who we are and who we're becoming. So may we be honest about both.

Even now, there are so many conflicting feelings and thoughts about the Vietnam War, but may we not let politics and biases get in the way of our passionate pursuit for our siblings and their well-being. We must be intentional about knowing one another's stories, about knowing where we've been and the sacrifices that have been made.

May we listen to the ground by remembering the stories because they still speak.

SO HOW DID Y'ALL MEET?

I was at a dinner party recently with some new friends. I'm on a board with many of these people, and we just don't know each other all that well. It seemed to me that if we were going to run a board together, we should also start getting to know one another and spend time with each other because so much of the impact of leadership happens through relationships. So, I was at this dinner party with my wife and my new friends and colleagues, and the classic question that often comes up at a table full of couples was asked: How did y'all meet?

So, everyone started telling their stories: about their first dates, their engagements, their weddings. As the night went on and we were sharing with each other we began to bond. We were laughing together, smiling together, crying together, feeling inspired together. It was just all the feels and the emotions, and I realized in that moment that I was finally getting to see these people on the inside. Over the course of this dinner, each of my colleagues became more real than just someone on the board whom I might see around an office. I began to really see them through their stories. Jimmy, who accidentally locked his fiancée in an outhouse while it was sixteen below at the cabin they were vacationing in, will now never look the same. I see him through this hilarious, embarrassing story, and it's brought us closer together. Laura is a different woman to me after I learned about her cancer and how her husband loved her back to health. Their beautiful story touched me, and I care for Laura with a new depth. Lindsey is a different man to me now that I've heard the story of his wife's passing and the memories he holds of her that are now marked with loss and tenderness. He will no longer be the intimidating, nonchalant, somewhat melancholy, and aloof CEO he was to me before. Now that we know each other better, I cannot unsee and unhear these people and their stories. It reminds me that there's something about learning how God has made and wired a person, how they have become who they are through their life experiences and challenges, that changes how we see, know, and ultimately love one another.

Knowing your yesterday shapes how I see you today, and how I show up for you tomorrow. It shapes how I respond and engage with you because the more I know you, the better I understand you, and the better I understand you, the more meaningful our relationship is. This whole idea is complex but it's also very simple.

When our church was first starting, we would do communion. Being new to California, I did not know "gluten-free" was such a thing. Before I came to SoCal, I'd honestly never even heard of gluten. But now I'm in California leading this young church, and there's this young woman who can't eat the crackers or bread we served at communion. Apparently, those crackers and bread were full of gluten, and she could not participate at the family table because of it. So, what did I do? Did I tell her to go somewhere else because here in this church we believe in gluten? Of course not. We just made adjustments—we did some research and got some gluten-free bread so this young woman could participate.

Over time, she really became a part of my family. She has been nannying for us for several years. We've watched her go through college, and we celebrate her now that she's a self-made businesswoman making waves in the world. She travels with us and vacations with us and, as I say, she's just a part of our family now. My family is known for hospitality, and we love cooking and having parties and sharing food. As this young woman began to get closer with us and we learned more about her—her story, her challenges and burdens—it started to shape our menu. Whenever she comes over, we make a point to cook in a way that includes her because for us to love her well and have her be an accepted, seen, and known member of our family, we have to pay attention to gluten and make sure we aren't serving her something she can't digest.

See, what I want you to understand is that as we learn more about one another, it changes how we show up and changes how we love. We begin making adjustments to include more at the table because we love them and want them there, and that's part of loving our siblings well.

I'll never forget being on a retreat with some of my church staff. Though they're my staff, these people are also some of my closest friends. While we were on this retreat we got to talking about injustices and things that challenge us and break our hearts. There was a young guy named Josh on staff, and he had a young son and daughter with Down syndrome. As we're all talking, he began to tell us about his kids, and he got emotional. With tears in his eyes and anger in his voice, Josh told us about how much he hates it when people throw around the word "retard" or the phrase "you're retarded." He talked about how he could never have respect for someone who used such vile, visceral language. He said it was the epitome of disrespect and disregard, and the thought of anyone referring to his children or anyone with that language was too much. In that moment, I saw a level of anger that was uncharacteristic of the man I knew, and it was clear that this anger was sending a message that said, "This is a very big deal to me."

While I was processing what he was saying, I started thinking about how, culturally, that word and phrase are used as casual slang. In fact, I've said it before in my own life. I wasn't currently using it in that season of my life, but as a young kid in middle school and high school? We used to say it all the time just casually. But in that moment as I was listening to my brother Josh, I was thinking about how I would never use that word again, nor let it be said by anyone in my presence without speaking up and calling it out. I thought to myself, "What would Josh think of me if I was sitting in spaces and with people using that word, knowing what it means to his son and daughter?" My loving Josh and being a good friend and sibling to him means that I have to adjust my language, my thoughts, and even my values so that they do not cause harm to him. I have to address my ignorance and my missed opportunities to be a better sibling and make the world an easier place for him and his family.

In that same conversation, another coworker and great personal friend told us about her sister who is a little person and how the word "midget" is extremely offensive. Again, I had that same experience: I know of people who have used that word and who still say it. To be totally transparent, I thought it was a legitimate expression for a little person and I had no idea how much hurt it brought to this community and to my friend and colleague's family specifically. Now hearing her experiences and her journey and learning that this word was used abusively toward her sister, I thought that there was no way I would ever again sit in a space where that word was being used and not call it out. Because of my love for my sister, I change how I speak, and the way others speak around me.

I guess what I'm trying to say is that if we're going to really love each other and be good siblings, we have to be willing to change our menus, our language, our hearts, and our biases. We have to be willing to change, period. And not based on our comfort or convenience but based on what our neighbors and siblings need. We have to see and lighten their burdens, rather than stand by our "rights" and not change, because there's something so much bigger happening here. God has made it abundantly clear that how we love one another matters. It's the two questions tied together: Where are you and where is your brother? How do you love God and how do you love your neighbor? Bottom line: We have to care.

I just want to take this moment to give us a reminder: Our love is how the world knows it's real. They will know we are Christians not by our doctrines or beliefs or even our theology—but by our love.

To love is to know the full story: the parts that are worthy of celebration and laughter and fun, and the parts that require mourning and lament. To love is to know it all and sit with each other in the highs and lows. Scripture tells us to rejoice with those who rejoice and mourn with those who mourn—it's just what good siblings do.

CELEBRATED, TRIGGERED, AND TRAUMATIZED

Election night, November 2007. I'm at home in our condo in Los Angeles with our two little girls, Zoe and Bethany. My wife, LaRosa, is at a women's group at our church. I'm glued to the TV, watching as they announce President-Elect Barack Obama. Let me tell you, I had a moment. I called my girls into the room and had them sit with me on my chair. With tears in my eyes, I held them close and told them, "Anything is possible, girls." Of course, they didn't quite understand and wanted to get back to whatever game they had been playing, but it was such a big night for me and so many others across this nation. It was a night of pride and celebration and hope. It was something we've never experienced before in this generation, and it was profound.

CELEBRATED

When President Obama was inaugurated in January 2008, I remember my mother, aunties, uncles, cousins, and siblings all piled into their cars and drove up to Washington, DC, to see the inauguration live and in person. I remember seeing the photos they sent me and posted on social media of them bundled up in scarves and coats and mittens because, being from Mississippi, they weren't at all used to the freezing temperatures in DC. It was a day of such joy to see the first Black president sworn into office, and my family made a point to go out of their way and be there to witness it.

Months later while I was visiting my mom at home, I was taken aback to walk into her house and see this huge poster-sized picture framed in gold of Barack and Michelle dancing together at the inauguration party. It's that iconic photo many of us have seen: Barack in his black tuxedo and Michelle in her stunning ball gown. This blown-up, nearly life-sized photo was hanging in Mom's den on full display. Just for some context, I've been married for many years. My wedding picture isn't even hung up like this for all to see in Mom's den.

So, clearly, this is a proud moment for her. It's a proud moment— not a political one. My mom's love for Barack and Michelle had and has nothing to do with politics, but everything to do with what they represent. To live to see a Black man voted into the presidential office has been cause for some of the most joy and celebration we've ever seen because so many of us know and have witnessed what white supremacy is capable of. In that moment of victory, we were suddenly able to see the ideal of America and what's possible when we all come together and rise above the worst part of our past and the greatest of our hopes. We were celebrating what was now possible—what so many Black people thought was impossible.

Looking back twenty, forty, sixty, one hundred, two hundred, four hundred years—could anyone have imagined this? Just think of a slave in the Middle Passage, coming on a ship to the southern states, forced to pick cotton and work for a master—could they ever have imagined there would be a Barack or Michelle Obama?

In the days of his victory, we celebrated simply because of what was now possible, not what was political. As we work toward the heart of racial reconciliation and becoming better siblings and people, we have to understand that there's a wider story we're experiencing that many of our white siblings can't see or choose not to see. After Obama's win, so many of my white Christian siblings came to my office in various stages of fear and dismay, saying that they didn't know how a Democrat could also be a Christian. They referenced all the babies they feared would inevitably be murdered under Obama's watch, all while failing to acknowledge that there were plenty of babies murdered on George Bush's watch. While the victory was still fresh, the conversation immediately turned political. And don't get it twisted—that's to be expected. This was an election, after all, and political discourse is right and understandable and needs to be had. But what so many of my white siblings missed is that we're living one big story as a people, and as such we mourn and experience joy and carry trauma and feel the weight of these emotions as a people. I know there are some siblings of color who opt out of that narrative—who say that they are not part of the collective and that not all trauma is their own. But even so, there are so many of us who see and experience these moments together, and Obama's victory spoke volumes about how far America has come in some regards. You have to understand that generations of people, of Black families, didn't think it was possible.

I threw a party with friends from all walks of life to celebrate Obama's win and what it means in the wider story. I can't stress enough that this was not a political celebration, but one to acknowledge and rejoice about what was now possible, about all that the ancestors lost and sacrificed to ultimately pave the way. If you went to many homes in early 2008, especially homes owned by Black people of a certain generation, you'd likely see Barack and Michelle up on many walls. And not because of their politics, but simply because they're our people and they've shown us what's possible—and that's worth celebrating.

TRIGGERED

It was the summer of 2020, and we were in the throes of pandemic anxiety. I'd already done a funeral over Zoom for someone who had died of COVID, my children were finishing up what had been a very hectic school year in which they had to transition to distance learning, and all around us there was just this tension marked with a low-grade fever of anxiety. As we watched the news every day for updates on COVID deaths, hospitalizations, and spread, we were also cleaning our groceries once we got them home, taking off clothes and taking multiple showers, and doing everything we could to stay inside and far away from the virus. I tell you; this was a time like no one had ever seen before in this generation. Suddenly, at the height of the pandemic and quarantine and this persistent anxiety, things reached a fever pitch: Ahmaud Arbery was chased down and killed by two white men while another white man followed with a camera and recorded the whole thing. As this footage came out, we were watching in disbelief. We were literally witnessing a Black man being hunted down. It had been only weeks since George Floyd, and now we're learning about Ahmaud, who had actually been killed in February 2020. We just didn't know his story or the details of his murder until more than three months later. Well, with all these racially charged hate crimes happening so close together, it created a level of uncertainty, devastation, and loss unlike anything we've ever seen. There was suddenly an outcry as people marched in the streets to protest what had happened as all of this was going on; I came down with a serious case of cabin fever.

With the world on fire outside, months of tension and fear while being stuck inside, and uncertainty about the future, I just needed a release. I needed to get out of the house and with my friends, back in community with my people. Soon, my guys and I had a group chat going and we'd planned a little hangout to just meet, connect, and breathe in the midst of everything that had been going on. So, I made a deal with my wife to go and see my friends: We'd all been tested, none of us had been anywhere except home and maybe the grocery store, and we were going to follow all the guidelines for gathering safely so we could just have a much-needed hangout.

Well, the day came, and I was ready to head out. I grabbed my keys and before I left the house, LaRosa gave me a hug with a little extra squeeze. Like, she was clinging to my neck just a little bit. She looked at me and, like she always does, she told me to be careful. Except, this time I was surprised to see this look in her eyes when she said it—they were different and intense, urgent. Her voice was different too—her telling me to "be careful" wasn't how it usually was, casual and easy. This time, it felt like more of a plea. I could hear the crackle in her voice and as she hugged me goodbye, she did so a little harder than usual.

I was headed out to Los Angeles where my friend lived, and it was just weird how empty the freeway was. I don't know how many of you know, but any day you can get out to Los Angeles and there's no traffic is a really good day (Cue Ice Cube for just a minute; can I get a witness?). So, I made it to my friend's house in record time and we just got to hang out, and it was exactly what I needed.

Now, one of the beautiful things about mine and LaRosa's marriage is that we both understand the importance and value of friends and community. So, we are intentional about encouraging one another to be with our friends and get into community. If she wants to go out with the girls, I tell her to set it up—bring them over, go grab some food, do an overnighter—whatever she needs, and she does the same with me. We do this because we know that when we each come back from being with our friends, we come back rejuvenated and better. We know that our respective friend groups are made up of godly men and women and that when we're with our friends, they make us better people. LaRosa comes back a happier, rejuvenated, and better wife, mother, and woman. I come back a better husband, father, and man. So, we don't have a marriage where we're constantly checking up on each other and asking, "Where are you?" or "What are you doing?" or "How long will you be gone?"

We just understand the necessity of our godly friend communities; iron sharpens iron. When she and the girls get together and when the guys and I get together, we're just iron coming together sharpening iron.

Well, that night was different.

Before I even got to my friend's house, I already had a text from LaRosa asking me if I made it. So, I texted her back and told her, "Yeah, babe, made it safely. Gonna have a good time!"

About an hour later, she texted me again and asked, "How's it going?" I was a little surprised, but I went ahead and wrote back that it was going well and we were having a ball. Around eleven o'clock, LaRosa sent yet another text. At this point, I was wondering what was up. As is the nature of most adult relationships, my friends are so spread out and so busy that we're only really able to get together once every few months. So, when we hang out, we hang out. We go all in with good conversation, good food, and fellowship. Sometimes we can be sitting up talking and hanging out until about one or two in the morning—and my wife knew this. So, to be perfectly honest, I was getting a little annoyed with all these texts. This time, she asked me what time I thought I'd be coming home, and honestly my reaction was irritation. I was thinking, "I can't really hang out with my guys because I've had to stay on the phone with you!" And it was just so abnormal. Usually, we give each other ample space, and this checking in was just not a thing.

Before I responded in the fullness of my irritation, I stopped and realized what was going on: It was eleven o'clock, her husband was in Los Angeles hanging out with his friends. As a Black man, he was about to drive about an hour home, and the number of things that could happen to a Black man driving through LA at midnight was just too high. We'd just seen some truly atrocious things happen to Black men who were out in broad daylight. So, there was a lot that could go wrong—too much that could happen. And it was just scary.

I realized at that moment that while I was having a nice time with my friends and getting this emotional exhale, my wife was at home holding her breath because she had been triggered. At that very moment, I understood that something was happening in her that I just hadn't noticed: She was a Black woman married to a Black man with two Black sons. What she'd been seeing on the news happening to men who look like her husband—what's been coming in from every direction—was filling her with fear. And what's important to note is that these were not isolated incidents. It wasn't just that Ahmaud Arbery happened to be killed and then, oh no! George Floyd happened to be murdered next! No, this had been happening for generations. This has happened to multitudes of unarmed Black men who were hung, beaten, burned, and abused. These are not isolated incidents—they are a string of incidents fueled by racism and hate, and they've triggered a reality across time of what white supremacy is capable of. Of how far it can and will go.

So, she asked when I was coming home, and it hit me that I needed to get my stuff together, tell the guys goodbye, and come home.

I'd later learn that LaRosa wasn't the only one who was triggered. Each of my friends' wives were worried as well. The mothers of Black sons and wives of Black men have all been triggered by this nation's present and past. America itself is triggered because once again it's been reminded of what white supremacists and systems are capable of. These are not isolated incidents, and we are not okay.

THE BLACK WOMAN

When I was in the seventh grade, my mom announced that there was a surprise baby coming. I was absolutely shocked. Truth be told, I didn't even know that could happen to my mom at her age (fast-forward many years later to my own wife getting pregnant and having our fourth child at that very same age). So, I was surprised but I was so excited for our little sister to come. It meant I'd no longer be the baby of the family and would have someone to push around and boss around—and, of course, someone to love and play with.

Well, I'll never forget one day being in PE class when the counselor came and got me and told me my sister was there to pick me up because there was an emergency. Apparently, Mom had gone into labor prematurely. During her pregnancy, she had developed preeclampsia and they had no choice but to take the baby out as soon as possible. At the time, I had no idea how sick my mom was because all the focus was on our baby sister. It wasn't until later that I found out just how dangerous a place she'd been in—we could have lost her.

After hours and hours of waiting, we finally got the news that our little sister Bethany had been born, but she was way too early. She was just a little over a pound in weight and she was so, so small. There was actually this little baby doll dressed in a blue dress and hat that we had bought for Bethany's nursery that we brought to the hospital for her. She and the doll were the same size. I'll never forget that image, how small she was.

So, for many days Bethany stayed in the NICU in this holding crib where she was totally intubated. Tubes were all over her little bitty nose, her heart, her hands, just her whole body. But she was moving. She had a long fight ahead, but she was moving.

As we were counting the days of her fight, the doctor came to us one day and said something I'll never forget. "Well," he said, "she's gonna need a miracle, but the thing that you've got going for you is that she's a Black girl. Hands down, Black girls are the strongest babies and they're fighters. So, she's strong, and your chances are better because she is a strong Black girl."

Unfortunately, even with all her strength and fighting, after about a month we had to say good night to Bethany with hopes of seeing her again in the eternal morning. But I never forgot what the doctor said about Black babies, girls, women, and their strength. As I got older, though, I had no idea that the term "Strong Black Woman" would be so weaponized against them, used to make them less human, easier to abuse, and easier to ignore when it comes to their pain and suffering. This term creates a notion that Black women are somehow superhuman, that they don't feel pain and fatigue in the same way. And this makes them a target for abuse and toxicity.

As I think about the ancestors who have gone before us, I can't help but stop and think about, and thank, the Black woman for all that it cost her so that we might be here today.

Dr. J. Marion Sims was an American physician considered to be the "godfather of modern gynecology." In the mid- to late 1800s, Sims was known for making strides and advancements in the field of surgery, and especially in women's health. A controversial figure, Sims has been credited with making great advances in women's medicine. However, it would soon become public knowledge that Sims was only able to perfect his research and surgical treatments and techniques by operating on enslaved Black women without anesthesia. This man would take enslaved Black women and literally experiment on their bodies at the expense of their pain and physical well-being. He would build an entire study that would ultimately accelerate the gynecological field, but it was all on the Black woman's body, pain, and torture. The Black woman was the foundation for this advancement, and while he was praised, too many Black women were used, abused, and killed on his watch and under his "care."[2]

In the twentieth century, he was stripped of his title and is now viewed as one of the most controversial figures in the history of medicine, but none of this comes close to atoning for the injustice he wrought and the blood he spilled. Oh, the price Black women were forced to pay for the gynecological advances that women across the world experience and benefit from today.

This brings to mind Henrietta Lacks.[3] She was a young Black mother who, in 1951, visited the John Hopkins Hospital (one of the few hospitals that would admit and treat poor Blacks) complaining of intense vaginal bleeding. She was examined by a renowned gynecologist, Dr. Howard Jones, who discovered a large, malignant tumor attached to her cervix. Over time, Mrs. Lacks underwent radium treatments, and a biopsy was taken of her tumor. The sample of her cancer cells was then sent to Dr. George Gey to be examined in his nearby tissue lab. For years, Gey had been collecting tissue samples from patients of John Hopkins Hospital, but they weren't fruitful. The sample cells would quickly die, but Mrs. Lacks's cells were different. Where other cells would expire, hers would double every day or so.

Today the cells, known as the HeLa cells, are still used to study the use and effect of different toxins, drugs, viruses, and hormones on the growth of cancer cells without doctors having to experiment on people. Over the decades these cells have been used to study the effect of radiation and poisons, study the human genome, develop the polio vaccine, and even learn how viruses work. Henrietta Lacks, though, died on October 4, 1951, at the young age of thirty-one. Her body is gone, but her cells have changed the world.

When I think about Mrs. Lacks, I think about how her body was used without her permission to do so much for so many. Though her cells are not literally superhuman, it has been scientifically confirmed that there's just something extremely special about those cells. In my own experience, I would say there's just something very special about the Black woman. But it comes at such a great and troubling cost. The Black woman identity is not a victim, but she's often victimized. She's special, but she's not superhuman.

I want to really sit in the reality of the fact that if not for the Black woman being abused excessively, we would not have these medical advancements across the globe—and that just doesn't sit right with me. Why has so much come at her detriment? At her expense? Why is her body not honored or given credit? It's absolutely barbaric, and it shows how much and how often Black women are left out of the conversation. While we talk of the Tuskegee experiments and those experiences of abuse and bodily injustice, the cries of Black women still go unheard. Even still today, the mortality rate of Black women in childbirth is significantly higher than white women and other women of color.

Carlos Whittaker shared a post on Instagram about how when Black women are in pain, they aren't given the same amount of medication that white women are given. Countless physicians chimed in on his post and confirmed and confessed that this is still true today. So many doctors still assume that Black women are stronger and therefore have a higher pain threshold than other women. Many Black women are so frustrated with the medical field because they are constantly unheard, misdiagnosed, and have had to say the same thing three or four times before they're taken seriously. The relationship between the medical world and the Black woman is one of the most abusive in the world.

Black woman, you are strong, but that is no excuse to be abused, used, or manipulated. It is no excuse to ignore your body, your humanity, your voice, or your cry. I thank you for your strength, Black woman. I thank you for your humanity, and I see it. Thank you for the sacrifice you had no choice but to make, Black woman. And through it all, thank you for your fierce love. May we give back to you all that has been taken.

TRAUMATIZED

It was time for my yearly checkup. I'd just tipped over forty years of age. My doctor was looking at my blood work when we had an alarming conversation. He told me they needed to put me on blood pressure medicine. Truth be told, that conversation was a marker of aging that I just wasn't ready for. I wasn't expecting it, and it honestly felt like it came out of nowhere. So, I immediately told my doctor I would start to eat better and exercise more and do the whole nine yards to ensure I stayed healthy. Well, my doctor did affirm that those were good and helpful choices, but he also asked me a question: "Did your father have high blood pressure?" I told him he did. Then he asked me, "Did your grandfather have high blood pressure?" I told him that Grandad did, too.

The doctor then told me that while eating well and exercising were good tools, I still might need the blood pressure medicine because the issue was in my genes. It was just something inherently inside of me passed down to me by my family members.

It honestly amazes me the things that can be passed from parent to child, and the list keeps growing. There's high blood pressure and alcoholism and things like that, but there's also trauma—generational trauma held in our bodies and passed down throughout time—especially in America. Because I am Black, there are things that are part of my story whether I want them to be or not. There are narratives and biases that have just been passed down to me whether I identify with them or not, whether I agree with them or not, and whether I want to acknowledge them or not. People of color swim in trauma like our white siblings swim in privilege. We are in it so deep that we don't even realize it's all around us. Sure, it can be worked through if we're determined, but the truth is that it takes so much time to do so.

It takes so long to untangle these knots that we can't afford to ignore them. So, we move through them together, as a family. Or at least, we should.

It's the realization that we're carrying something heavy, and we never really knew it. In these moments of racial upheaval and Black deaths, I have become so suddenly aware of the burden I have been carrying. I'm so blessed to have my Black male friends to gather and sit with so that we might hold and lament this trauma because it is so heavy at times, and so often it is unnoticed. It reminds me of when LaRosa and I are watching a scary or intense or suspenseful movie. Oftentimes, we get so caught up in the story and what's going to happen next—when the murderer is about to be revealed or when the verdict is about to be announced—that we often have to look at each other and remind one another to breathe.

When you're watching something that's hard, sometimes you hold your breath. It's just something we do. People of color, though, tend to do the same thing when walking through something hard, and we have to remind ourselves to breathe. Trauma makes us hold our breath, but we cannot hold it forever.

So, through the trauma, breathe.

Through racist attacks, breathe.

Through systemic racism, breathe.

Through fears, breathe.

Through injustice, breathe.

Through the indifference of siblings who say they love us but don't show up, breathe.

The question soon becomes whether our white siblings are willing to breathe through it with us or not. There's a need for a safe place to exhale fear, hurt, and hate. In that exhale, we need to inhale the hope and healing and love that help us make it through another day. This is something only God can provide, but I believe God has chosen to provide it through His children as well as through Himself. He has chosen to usher in salt, light, and love through His children, and so it's through our love for our siblings and enemies that healing is brought into the world.

So again, it begs the question: Am I my brother's keeper? Am I a bearer of hope, light, salt, justice, and love? The answer is yes. It has to be yes.

What I hear most from my Black siblings in moments of lament is something so hard yet so simple. In the midst of injustice, we hear it echoing throughout the corridors of time: I can't breathe.

So we long for spaces in and marked by the presence of Our Father. We long for spaces that are covered in grace, marked with justice, and overwhelmed by love where we can all breathe, where our trauma can be healed, and our triumphs celebrated. We want to breathe.

May we provide those spaces for one another in Jesus' name.

SIBLINGS OF COLOR

I'll never forget when my mentor and great friend, Bryan Loritts, had a conference on racial reconciliation called the KAINOS Conference in Memphis, Tennessee. The speakers there were phenomenal as they outlined racial injustices and how God calls the church to respond. I had the great privilege of being the host of the event that year, so it was up to me to keep the speakers coming and the show going, with ease and charisma, of course. One of the speakers was Soong-Chan Rah, this prolific Asian preacher who just has a way of moving the room he's preaching in, and the soul. He would say difficult, hard-to-swallow truths that cut like a knife but that were drenched in theological accuracy and academic prowess. No one could deny the substance of his words; even if you didn't like them, you had to respect them because he was just that good.

Well, at this conference Soong-Chan Rah came up to speak and he started talking about the attack on the Black family. He talked of the Middle Passage and how on that harrowing journey many would die: Some would jump overboard; others would die of exhaustion and illness. Some people were chained to those who had died, and so for the duration of the journey they had to stay shackled to a corpse. Once these ships made port, families were ripped apart and separated on the auction block, masters raped slave women and abused the men and children, beating them and selling them at the slightest whim. Families were utterly torn asunder and completely destroyed. Through all of that, though, the Black family still exists today, and it is a modern miracle. Soong-Chan Rah noted that because of all the Black family has been through, the very fact that it perseveres is a modern-day miracle. The fact that we are still able to come together and stay together is a testimony in and of itself.

As Soong-Chan was saying all of this, I was standing offstage having never felt more seen as a Black man by someone who doesn't look like me. When he was finished preaching, the room was rent with applause, and there was this clear public acknowledgment that, yes, the Black family has come through so much, through such an enormous array of obstacles. We are a modern miracle when one stops to think about all that has been done to eradicate us, yet we survive.

I felt so seen and so deeply moved in that moment, and as I returned to the stage, something landed within my soul that, unfortunately, came out as a joke. It was more true than I cared to admit at the moment, but it struck me then that this Asian man just spoke about me and my people in a way that brought me into an awareness of myself. He helped me see and understand myself; he spoke of me in such a way of care and compassion and dignity that I simply felt so loved. He saw me, and I felt that love and immediately recognized the deficit in my soul from the absence of that love in other parts of my life. At the time, all I could squeeze out was a joke. I said, wow, this man knows more about my culture than I do, and my only understanding of his culture stops at *The Karate Kid*! That got a big laugh, but in my own soul it was a confession of a deep, deep truth: I have made so much about Black issues and my own narrative about growing up in Mississippi that I know almost nothing of my Asian siblings or their story or their journey.

How can I love my Asian siblings well when I'm walking in such a deep, embarrassing ignorance of their story? At that moment I knew I had to be better and do better, and not just because it was right, but because it made me aware of how much I was missing God. To know my sibling's story and journey with God, to know how they engage with Him and experience Him, shapes my understanding of them and God. It's not just about being right or politically correct—it's about missing a huge part of the family of faith, of God's family. I've been living in my own comfort, experience, and pain for so long that I haven't done my due diligence to hear the stories of my Asian siblings.

That day, I began the process and the hard work of learning the stories. I've come a long way, but I feel like I've only just begun. But oh, what a joy to see and hear their stories and burdens—to know them better so I might love them better.

In 2020, we saw a rise in Asian hate. We saw political leaders taunt and poke at Asian people to use them as a scapegoat for the coronavirus, and it resulted in spreading fear and hate toward our Asian siblings. It was absolutely sick and wrong, and it has caused so much hurt and damage. See, regardless of whether the first instance of COVID was traced to a location in China, hate crimes are going up and this rhetoric is being weaponized against Asians, and it has to stop. Even if—and I'm being generous here—even if talking about China started only as a reference to where the virus originated, it has mutated beyond that. Where did "Kung Flu" come from? What do we see as a result of this inflammatory language? Abuse, assault, murder. Love says that we change our language, that we stop hate from being spread. It's not just about learning one's story, it's about hearing their burden and fighting with them to break it. My Asian siblings, I'm sorry it took me so long to get to the party, but I am finally here, and I'm ready to unlearn and learn.

When I first came to California, my role at my church was the youth pastor. Coming from the South where there were mainly whites and Blacks, this acted as my first introduction to the Latino community here in SoCal. In my new home and position, I was suddenly going to my first quinceñera, Christmas celebration with tamales, and all sorts of cultural events with my Latino siblings. I know a young Latina woman, Mayra, who is honestly like family to me now. Back then she would invite me and my family to these events all the time. The more I went to them, the more I realized how many of the burdens and issues in the Latino community were lost on me. I can hardly articulate the level of ignorance I was walking in daily. I soon learned that one of the biggest issues for this community was immigration and "illegal immigrants."

To be honest, coming from Mississippi my understanding of immigration was very limited and very black-and-white, cut-and-dried. I was unaware of the nuances of such stories, and my level of ignorance was honestly just so, so embarrassing. With this community, I hadn't asked, "Where is my brother?" or thought about it at all. Well, while I was doing this youth ministry in the church, our annual trip to Mexico was coming up, and this year we suddenly had to cancel. This thriving, mostly white church had a robust Mexico outreach ministry and had for many years. As the neighborhood surrounding the church began to change over the years, however, the youth groups were soon filled with more and more Latino kids, so the trip to Mexico was problematic. You see, so many of our kids had come to the United States as children, and their parents weren't citizens. Crossing the border was a dangerous thing for them, so as a church, we made the decision to cancel the trip and to do only trips that all our kids could go on safely and return.

Over time, one of our kids—let's call him Anthony—got the passion to become a pastor and so, as he grew up and got ready to go off to college, we worked with him to get him ready for this career path. Well, he was all ready to go off to the local Christian college, but there was one problem: Anthony was undocumented and brought here by his parents as a child. At the time, it was basically impossible for him to pay for school, because undocumented children can't apply for financial aid. But we couldn't leave him under this burden. So, the church gathered around him to help, and that process really forced me to see our immigration laws differently. It forced me to see how these laws are inherently filled with bias and are used to play a game of political football with real lives. Anthony was viewed by the government as having less value than documented or native US children, all because he was undocumented. He was seen as worth less than American kids because of a choice his parents made to give him a better future.

Well, long story short, we were able to pull some strings and raise some funds and get Anthony in school. He was off to college, and my eyes were freshly opened to the reality of the burdens my Latino siblings carry—and my ignorance about all of them. I also learned that understanding these burdens was on me, not them. It was not and is not the responsibility of the marginalized to explain why and how they're marginalized. It is not up to them to educate others on their burdens and raise our emotional quotient. That responsibility falls to us. We are capable of doing the research, asking the questions, reading the books, watching the discussions, and doing the work so that we might understand our siblings better. They are not responsible for our ignorance—we are.

To my indigenous brothers and sisters, I have to say I am so sorry. I honestly feel like I am today years old when I learn more about your story and your experiences in America. When I think about what I was taught about Native Americans in school, it is a disservice to the reality of what you and your ancestors have gone through. The abuse, rape, murder, and disease inflicted on our Native American siblings is ignored. The blood on the ground is crying out, but we aren't hearing it because their history was written by the hunters and the conquerors. It is time to hear from the hunted. We have not seen nor heard the whole story, and we are so late to the game. America was indeed built on the backs of slaves, but it was first stolen through the rape and robbery of our Native American siblings, and that is worthy of our outrage, our respect, and our recognition. We must learn the truth about the birth of America in order to understand where we actually come from. We must not learn from the hunter anymore, but the hunted—because their story is the one that matters, the one that cries out from the ground.

With our Armenian brothers and sisters, there is even more that I don't know. But living in SoCal and being surrounded by these siblings has brought me the joy of learning about them and their story, of being in fellowship with them. I remember sitting in the backyard with Armenian friends and learning their stories, sharing their food, and learning of their homeland, their ancestors, their sacrifice, and their genocide. In the spring of 2021, at the onset of the uprising in

Turkey,[4] it was such a privilege and blessing to sit with these same siblings and just be with them through it. Even in the midst of listening and advocating, and what often feels like the small action of posting on social media, there is such a power in just being with your siblings and sitting with them in their pain.

However, there's a young girl at our church named Julie whom I feel I've failed. Julie was in high school when the church began, and now she's a teacher and a passionate activist. She uses her classroom as a space to teach her students about justice and people—when the racial uprisings during the summer of 2020 began, she was out there protesting, one of the first to individually declare that "Black Lives Matter." But when the uprising began against her people and she was mourning, we did not love her well. We did not show up and it had a devastating effect. What was happening was a headline to us, but she was courageous enough to call us out and say that her family, her siblings, were not there for her. It's not just happening in Turkey—it needs to be happening in our hearts. We have to come together because our absence can become a burden.

I'm so thankful for Julie and her honesty about where I and the church fell short. I am so thankful for relationships that take me out of my own mind and push me into a wider perspective. Julie, my Armenian sister; Anthony, my Latino brother; my Asian siblings; and Native American siblings—my family of faith need me to stand just as I need them to. May we be there for one another, ready to do the hard work.

To all my siblings, I see you, and it is my hope that over time we will all learn to see one another and love better.

HOW WE OVERCOME

Whether it's the rows of flowers and signs and stuffed animals at the George Floyd memorial or the list of names on the Vietnam Veterans

Memorial, it's clear that forgetting is not an option. Not only should we remember their names, but we should say them out loud and tell their stories.

Let's go back and get what has been forgotten and omitted. We have to tell the whole story: the lynchings, the burnings, the genocides, those who have risked their lives to cross borders, those who have died, those Native Americans who were here from the start and were killed, all the blood soaked into the soil. May we not pick up the strategy of only telling one side of the story, for if we do this, there is no healing. Half the story cannot bring the whole healing we need for true reconciliation. So, let's go back, back to the Garden, so that we might answer the second fundamental question with integrity.

We are our brother's and sister's keeper. As siblings in Christ, we stand in hope of the cross and the blood of the lamb, but may we never ignore the blood on the ground. One does not outweigh the other; one does not replace the other. In Scripture, God asks the Israelites to remember, remember, remember. So let us remember.

Our past is not bondage, it is a testimony to God's faithfulness. The Book of Revelation tells us that these are they that have overcome by the blood of the lamb and the words of their testimony, so let us testify of our journey, of where we've been, of the good and the bad and all the stories in between to the faithfulness of God. Because we are still here. We are still here!

We are washed by the blood of the lamb so that we might tell the story of the blood on the ground.

CHAPTER 7

DEAR AMERICA

NOT A WORSHIP SONG

A very good friend of mine is the pastor of a multiethnic church down in Texas, and one of his congregants is a very well-off white woman who holds this annual event. It's a pretty big fund-raising event, and it ultimately translates to being a gathering of her conservative friends and colleagues. Now, when I say "conservative friends and colleagues," I don't just mean some of her neighbors who vote like her. No, this party is adorned by Republican celebrities—speakers and public servants whom you would regularly see on Fox News. Among the who's who of the party guests, a prominent member of the GOP is always chosen to be the keynote speaker for this event.

Needless to say, this star-studded affair is marked by a pretty strong partisan presence.

Well, my pastor friend is also a Black man, and one year he was invited to this gathering to pray. To be clear, by his own admission my friend is an independent, so he wasn't invited because he belongs to any political party. The way he saw it, he was invited and would attend because he was a pastor serving one of his members who requested his presence—no more, no less. So, as my friend was getting ready to go to this event, he admitted that he didn't really know what he was getting into. Once there, he immediately noticed he was recognizing a lot of faces—many of the guests were people he'd actually seen speaking on Fox News and other outlets. It was surreal, but it was just the beginning. When the program began, he went up to the podium, said a prayer over the crowd, and then returned to his seat. As he was sitting down, music started playing: "God Bless the U.S.A." by Lee Greenwood. In fact, Lee Greenwood himself had taken the stage and begun leading the room in song.

As my friend told me about this experience, he stressed that what happened next was unlike anything he'd ever seen before. All around him people were crying, slowly standing and singing, raising their arms in unrestrained praise. Though he'd just said a prayer, my friend was taken aback by all of this because he was literally sitting in the middle of a worship experience—except worship music wasn't playing. These guests, though, were having a moment. The physical and emotional responses they were showing were making it clear just how moved they were by the song (and, dare I say, the Spirit?). This was not just a song to them; it was worship, and they truly were proud to be Americans.

"It was unlike anything I have ever seen," he said again and again.

But personally? I think we see it all the time.

As we talk about America and race, we have to talk about one of the biggest areas that divides us and gets in the way of having an open and honest dialogue: rampant patriotism. "God Bless the U.S.A." is not a worship song. But too often we see that many people view patriotism in a way that makes it entirely exclusive, which in turn makes it toxic. What I mean is that for many white Americans, American pride often looks and feels like worship, and most people of color just do not have that relationship with America. For too long, America has been the perpetrator of wanton abuse on marginalized communities and people of color. With this truth constantly hanging over the heads of people of color, it becomes very hard to feel that America is worthy of our worship, let alone any worship at all.

Now, I want to be clear: None of this is to say that people of color are not proud Americans. I will go on record to say that we are for sure proud Americans, but we are not always proud of who America is and what it does. Don't get it twisted: Though we don't find America worthy of worship, we are indeed proud Americans. We're proud of the ideals and hopes of America, of the freedom it stands for. Trust me, I have been all over the world and I have seen firsthand how privileged we are in America. We are free to do and be what we choose, and that's something to celebrate. But the differences between being a proud American and being a "patriot" are many and clear.

The word "patriot" can be pretty loaded. It creates this division because "patriot" can quickly begin to look like waving rebel flags and participating in toxic nationalism that leads to superiority, which makes life harder and scarier for people of color—for me personally as a Black man. With this said, I want to create and talk to a different kind of patriot—the kind of patriot worth making room for.

When I think about Black people and what we've contributed to this land and the investments we've made, you cannot tell me we aren't proud to be Americans. The toil, the sweat, and yes, the blood are all markers of the contributions and investments we've made here—many voluntarily, and many against our will. When I think about all we've contributed to our culture and who we are as individuals—post office workers, police officers, firefighters, military, and so on—it becomes clear that Black men and women have always been part of the fabric of this country. Collectively we have poured into it, invested in it, and even fought for it—without much recognition and often met with even more abuse.

I would go as far to say that people of color are true patriots because we constantly invest in and fight for a country that has not been willing to fight for us. In a 2017 report from the Equal Justice Initiative, entitled "Lynching in America: Targeting Black Veterans," a poignant quote from Chad L. Williams on the subject is shared:

> If African Americans learned a lesson from the experiences of Black combatants and noncombatants, it was to never again underestimate the depths of racial bigotry and its ability to pervert the ideals the nation supposedly fought for.[1]

History tells us that the military legacy of African Americans began with the arrival of the first enslaved Africans and spans to the present day. Black Americans were both drafted and welcome to enlist to fight in every war the United States has fought in or was a part of, from the Revolutionary War to the War in Iraq. The 163 units of Black soldiers in the Civil War, the Allied armies of both World Wars, the Tuskegee Airmen of the 332nd Fighter Group—hundreds of Black Americans stepped up to fight and volunteered to join the military time and again. Even so, the U.S. armed forces were segregated through World War I, and Black veterans were subjected to abuse, such as eating in the rain, no access to toilets, sleeping in tents without floors, and having no facilities in which to wash their clothes or bathe.[2] Black bodies have always been good enough to fight and die for this country, but not to be honored by this country during wartime or upon their return home, where many were lynched.

The EJI report says:

No one was more at risk of experiencing violence and targeted racial terror than Black veterans who had proven their valor and courage as soldiers during the Civil War, World War I, and World War II. Because of their military service, Black veterans were seen as a particular threat to Jim Crow and racial subordination.[3]

So, yes, we are true patriots, but a different kind.

Part of our ability to talk about America and race is to acknowledge that this has been an abusive relationship from the start: from the slave trade on African shores, to the years of Jim Crow, to redlining and police brutality, to unfair banking systems that keep people of color away from any upward mobility, to lack of equity and equality in schools, to the classroom-to-prison pipeline. This has been an abusive relationship, and we have to talk about the impact the abuse has had on generations of Black Americans. The trauma of this abuse stays with each and every one of us; it lingers and remains close.

So, when we talk about America, it's not about lacking appreciation, healthy patriotism, or even pride for our country. It's just that the lack of understanding of this abusive relationship and the impact it continues to have is not something we can be silent about or overlook anymore. We have to acknowledge these ugly facts as part of the relationship so that we can talk about them, move forward, and heal from them.

The way to bring healing and wholeness to an abusive relationship is to work through the past so that we might have a future free of inauthenticity, secrets and lies, bitterness, and further abuse. We have to tell the truth about what has happened, about the abusers and the systems that still perpetuate them. We have to talk about these dynamics as a people and a country, and to ignore this opportunity is to ruin our opportunity for hope and healing in our future.

PREFERRED PROTEST

Oh, the stories we tell of history.

When I think about Dr. King and the civil rights movement and all the daily disruption they caused, I find it utterly amazing how we speak of them now in our day and age. It's as if those were the glory years of our fight and our hope. We celebrate Dr. King and his speech and his dream, but we seem to forget that it all happened just a little more than fifty years ago. I don't know about you, but that makes me wonder: Who were the people fighting them? Who were the people opposing them? Where are they now? And how strong and violent was the opposition that the movement had to fight so incredibly hard?

Today, the marches are so celebrated when just a generation ago, they were opposed. I guess the point I'm trying to make is that it wasn't that long ago. Many of those who opposed Dr. King have children and grandchildren and families still alive today. Yet we have this way of telling history that sets America up to consistently be the hero and the savior—as if what Dr. King and the movement were fighting wasn't America itself. When we look back on those days now, we talk about them in a very watered-down way—we talk about slavery and then move on to Dr. King as if everything is fixed now and all right, as if it's all over and overcome.

Oh, the stories we tell of our history.

You see, how we tell our stories shapes our ability to heal from them. So, we have to tell the truth about what happened to us, and we have to tell the truth about what we did. And in this truth telling the goal is not shame or guilt or discomfort—it's simply truth. We cannot not tell the truth because we worry it will make white people uncomfortable or feel bad. When we've been in an abusive relationship, we cannot not talk about the abuse simply because it makes the abuser feel bad. To do so is to miss a greater opportunity for healing and restoration—and we cannot get there if we let discomfort and guilt hold our tongues. We cannot let discomfort and guilt hold our healing hostage.

I'm reminded of when I did an interview with a white journalist from a Christian magazine a few years ago. During my interview we got to talking about Colin Kaepernick and his kneeling at football games during the national anthem.

Now, we know that kneeling was his way of using his platform to peacefully protest the unjust killings of Black men at the hands of police. When he started this protest, he simply wouldn't rise for the anthem. He would sit down on the bench. But after backlash from veterans, he was advised that sitting down made it appear too much like he was disrespecting the sacrifice countless veterans have made for the flag. Well, of course, Kaepernick said that was not at all his intention, so he changed his stance and began to kneel rather than sit to be more respectful of the sacrifice and still acknowledge his protest. If you were around and paying attention during that time, you know that everyone just about lost their mind over this. People thought it was the most disrespectful thing they'd ever seen, and Kaepernick still hasn't fully recovered from the backlash.

Well, as I was talking about this with the white journalist for this Christian magazine, the journalist said something so profound it has stuck with me all this time later. He said, "You know what, I agree with what Colin is doing and I get what he's trying to say, but he's just protesting the wrong way. I just think that kneeling during the National Anthem is the wrong way to protest."

Unfortunately, I soon found that many of my white siblings felt the same way as this journalist: It wasn't the protest, necessarily, it was how it was executed—which was the wrong way. But it made me think: If we were to go back to that time and really experience the Civil Rights movement again, and not the sanitized version we think about now, would my white siblings be willing to acknowledge the truth of what white Christian leaders were saying then? Because, roughly, it's all the same.

What the journalist and many of my white siblings were saying was "I prefer you protest in another way. Kneeling is not the right way to protest." And then came Black Lives Matter, and that was an even worse way to protest. To make things even harder, that phrase alone— Black Lives Matter—is so controversial because of the organization it's attached to and the reaction it brings out of people. You hear "Black Lives Matter!" and you can be sure to hear "All lives matter!" hurled back with venom and frustration. In addition, the Black Lives Matter movement and organization contain elements that are, for lack of a better phrase, outside of theological correctness, and people reject it even more. People don't believe what the organization believes, and they're not fighting for much of what the organization is fighting for. But this complicates the simple declaration that Black Lives do Matter, and it all becomes problematic. But at the same time, isn't "Make America Great Again" the same? Is it not tied to organizations and practices that are undoubtedly outside of God's will, Christian ethics, and theological correctness?

Still, there's this resounding refrain that some white siblings would rather their siblings of color protest another way. Walking the streets at rallies, protesting online and in person—all of this is wrong to them, and they end up having more compassion for burned buildings than for murdered bodies.

"I prefer you protest another way."

More recently there has been an onslaught of criticism for critical race theory even though it's clear that most people don't even know what it is. For the record, critical race theory is an academic concept that's more than forty years old.[4] The main idea is that racism is a social construct and not just the result of individual biases and prejudice—it is something built into our legal systems and policies, and it works to keep people of color at a perpetual disadvantage in this country. So, when it comes to the examination of laws and policies that shape our country, this theory suggests that race is critical. While it's nice to have the definition, I would go so far as to say that this push against critical race theory is really another attempt by some white siblings to say, "I prefer you find another way to protest and express your frustration."

See, I keep coming back to Dr. King and the white Christian leaders of his day. Dr. King is so celebrated today, but back then those Christian leaders sent him correspondence while he was in Birmingham Jail that said, in essence, "We prefer you protest another way. Put this movement on hold because it's costing too much and creating too much division. Now is not the time." But Dr. King responded in his letter from the Birmingham jail[5] saying that he hoped they, like some of their white brothers who had been acting as allies to Dr. King and the civil rights movement, "recognized the urgency of the moment and sensed the need for powerful 'action' antidotes to combat the disease of segregation." In the film *The Great Debaters*,[6] Jurnee Smollett in her portrayal of Wiley College debate team member Henrietta Bell Wells shares the sentiment thus: "The time for justice...is always right now!"

There has often been so much opposition to this conversation, especially from some white, and I would even add evangelical, siblings, when it comes to the abusive relationship between America and people of color since the very beginning. The need for justice is now, but when I look at some of my white siblings and their actions, it's clear that it's not about how we protest or the right time for it, it's that we're protesting at all—it's that we're talking about the abuse at all— and they don't want us to. They don't want us to talk about our pain in any way that moves them to talk about it with us because of the guilt, discomfort, and shame it brings.

Which forces me to ask the question: What's your preferred form of protest? How do you recommend your siblings of color go after this systemic problem that perpetuates the abusive relationship we've been stuck in for centuries? How do you prefer we protest? Because for us, silence is not an option. Anything less than justice is not an option.

So, I ask you again: What's your preference?

THESE YOUNG PEOPLE

Several years ago, I was having a conversation with my goddaughter, and she was lamenting about her college experience. You see, she was attending a majority-white Christian college, and she was frustrated with some of the issues on campus and how she was being treated during the day-to-day: people touching and asking rude questions about her hair, asking questions about where she's really from, making assumptions about the kind of music she listens to and the food she eats. As I was listening to her, I was just trying to encourage her, and in doing so I discovered a generational gap that ultimately served me well and brought a whole new perspective to my life.

When she was telling me all of this, my first thought was really, "Well, what did you expect? You went to a white institution, and this is just how they are." I told her the best thing she could do was just get her degree and then get out of there! Don't try to change the world or the college, just get her degree and change her own life. If I'm being honest, all of her issues, while definitely annoying, appeared so small to me. I didn't see why she was sweating them, especially when that's just how things are. Well, in her response, she introduced me to a new word: microaggressions.

All those little annoying things have a name.

The dictionary describes "microaggression" as:

- a statement, action, or incident regarded as an instance of indirect, subtle, or unintentional discrimination against members of a marginalized group such as a racial or ethnic minority.
- indirect, subtle, or unintentional discrimination against members of a marginalized group.[7]

To me, these little moments never had a name. They were just a thing that happened, especially in majority-white spaces. So, when I asked my goddaughter, "Well, what did you expect?" I was amazed when she responded, "I expected freedom. Freedom from daily having to be an educator of my culture, from having to live in dorm rooms where I feel abnormal and othered, freedom from micro- and macroaggressions."

I realized at that moment that I didn't expect freedom from white institutions. I didn't expect these white spaces to understand or acquiesce to my experiences or my right to freedom. Why would I?

For me, I get along with my white siblings through building community. I've seen change and things I would never expect from my white siblings in that community. I saw it as separate, as an intentional space where siblings go to learn more about each other and be better. But I soon realized that I did not hold this same expectation for white institutions and systems. This was the moment I saw the difference between us: I didn't expect anything, but my goddaughter expects the white institutions to change and be better.

I see now that many in my generation and I have just accepted

153

the wins of the Civil Rights movement and the opportunities we now have access to as enough. We have access to spaces our ancestors did not and now we can get our degrees, get out, and pursue our own upward mobility. For so long my mindset has been "These white folks are going to be white folks and these institutions are going to be these institutions. I know they don't care about me and I'm not expecting them to move away from this culture of whiteness that serves them." I've been able to work through the barriers over what these places are, and what they are not, and I've just never expected them to be better. The comments, the cultural insensitivity, the microaggressions—all of that is what my generation and I learned to live with. But my god-daughter and her friends—a group of millennials—were not having that. They want better and they expect more.

A good friend of mine is the pastor of a multiethnic church, and he's been in multiethnic ministry for many, many years. He's a Black man and his son, who's about twenty years old now, is half Black and half Latino. Well, I was talking to this friend recently when his son suddenly called. He picked up the phone and his son immediately said, "Dad, I just left church." My friend said okay and asked his boy how it was, and his son said, "I don't know. I had to get out of there before the sermon was over. This is the last time I'm going to a white evangelical church."

Immediately, I got it. At that moment, my friend's son was expressing something that, to me, needs no explanation. I know it and most people of color know it. Do a quick Google search of "POC and white evangelical churches," and you'll see rows and rows of headlines about racism among white Christians, Black churchgoers quietly leaving white churches, and talk of an "exodus" of people of color from white churches that continue to harm and mistreat their siblings. People of color all over the country are fed up with dealing with the microaggressions that come with the white evangelical church. They refuse to live and worship in spaces where there is so much cultural insensitivity and cultural incompetence. My friend's son refused to be a token at this church, brought in as part of an experience, when the church itself wouldn't change its experience so that it seamlessly included people like him and those who look like him without making them feel othered. He was done being in spaces driven by toxic nationalism and hyper conservatism. Done with this view of America that time and again refuses to engage in the reality of its abusive history or acknowledge the ongoing injustices and imperfections. And I want to be clear: It's not that people of color want to live in the past or stay and dwell in these hurts. Acknowledgment does not mean parking the car. But it does mean that these harmful dynamics that have been in play shaping the current experiences of millions of people of color are seen, and by being seen they'll hopefully be dealt with.

My friend's son wanted what many believers of color want: a worship experience that speaks to where he is and what he's going through in his social location. He was frustrated with the church's inability to provide this, and it just wasn't worth staying in that space.

What's so interesting about all of this is that he was recommended to this church by his dad! His dad, my friend, thought this was a multiethnic church, and so he told his son about it and encouraged him to go.

"Dad," his son said, "did they actually tell you they were multiethnic?" My friend said yes, they did! And then his son said something so powerful: "Well, they lied."

My millennial goddaughter, my friend's Gen Z son—these young people are refusing to settle and be complacent. They're refusing to say, "We don't expect more from white institutions, white America, and the white church." They are refusing to settle for what they can get, like many in my generation and I have. They are refusing to settle for just upward mobility.

It's like the person who's been in an abusive relationship so long that they've been dehumanized and devalued and internalized that as truth. Like the abused, we can no longer see our own self-worth or what we deserve, and so we don't expect much and settle for even less. And the kicker? We actually think that what we're settling for is better than what we used to have—that it's not as bad as it used to be!

Friends, I believe that my goddaughter and these younger generations—these millennials and Gen Zs—are reminding us all that we should expect more. We should expect more from our white siblings and these white institutions. We should expect full freedom and refuse to accept anything less.

AMERICANITY

Tim Kuhl, a dear friend of mine who works at Southwest Church down in Indian Wells, California, and I were recently talking about nationalism, America, and Christianity, and the dangerous act of them all coming together. Really light conversation, I know. As we were talking, Tim used a made-up word that just encapsulates what we were talking about and the danger within it: Americanity.

It's like this: If politics and Christianity got together and had a baby, the unholy offspring would be Americanity and it is a dangerous, dangerous thing.

Americanity is the Bible that has taken American history and the Constitution and tried to weave them together into one entity. It's the cross in front of your church paralleled by the American flag—way too close for comfort. It's the not-so-subtle suggestion that America and Christianity are on the same level and go together hand in hand. It is the dangerous act of integrating the cross and the flag and making them one. In short, it's the worship song that is not a worship song, and it's all about a warped nationalism that puts America on the same level as the kingdom of God.

The most dangerous things about Americanity are its idols: the donkey and the elephant. We get so caught up in these representations of our political parties that we forget we don't worship at the altars of donkeys or elephants—we're called to worship only at the altar of the Lamb.

The reality of the Republican and Democratic parties is that they both have agendas, and these agendas shape the fight for a greater America. But the problem with these parties and their agendas is that Jesus Christ, the body of Christ, and Christianity as a whole do not fit under the elephant or the donkey. The word of God will not and cannot be found holistically under either of these agendas. So if God cannot be fully found under these agendas, how is it that so many are comfortably nestled and tucked in under the labels of "Democrat" and "Republican"?

This is the problem with Americanity: We create our own version of the Bible so that it fits the profile of our political party, and we end up missing the profile of the lamb, which is the kingdom of God. We have to understand and then resist the temptation to fit our theology, way of life, understanding of God, and doctrine under a donkey or an elephant. Why? Because we don't fit! We won't fit! So, if you find yourself comfortably fitting you and your faith in your political party, therein lies a huge problem.

What we need to understand is that the biggest problem with elephants and donkeys is that too many of us are so devoted and committed to something that will never offer up their life for you. They will not usher in the freedom for all that the gospel inevitably does and will do. You cannot give your life to something that won't die for you, and the elephant won't, and neither will the donkey. But the lamb? The lamb will die for you, has died for you, and actively does the opposite of what both the elephant and the donkey do, which is divide and degrade. They are not seeking to restore anyone or anything outside of their agenda. They are protecting their lives at all costs, and they are always going to preserve their agenda, their perspective, and their ideology at all costs, even if it requires them to be dishonest about what's actually happening, even if it means they create their own personal truth through their narrow lens and perspective. The elephant and the donkey are all about self-preservation, and each will hold views that can be antithetical to the gospel. So, while we participate in political parties, our allegiance cannot be to our political party; it has to be exclusively and wholly to the lamb of God.

Growing up in the South, most of my family and friends were Democrats. Most Black people I knew were Democrats. As I grew and matured in my faith, however, I began to understand and recognize that there are many things within the Democratic Party that fall outside of God's agenda. So, the alternative was to become a Republican, but there were concerns there, too. Parenthetically, I want to be clear that I am both liberal and conservative. I believe that the Bible is both. In my life I have voted for both liberals and conservatives, and can I tell you something? I've been disappointed each time. So, many years ago I declared myself as an independent because I see the word of God as independent itself. I identify with issues on both sides: There are conservative concerns that I stand with, support, and will fight for. At the same time, there are liberal concerns that I stand with, support, and will fight and vote for. I guess what I'm trying to say is that the word of God calls us at times to live in both worlds.

If you put an unrealistic, deistic hope in either party, they're going to disappoint you. And what I've found that's most unsettling is that the left largely wants to run from the throne of God, while the right wants to sit on it. But God is calling us to surrender to the throne and follow the fullness of His agenda.

Maybe it goes without saying, but my hope is not in Americanity. This nationalized, toxic version of Christianity, where the cross is wrapped up in the American flag, can bring us nothing good.

My hope, then, is in the throne of God where the cross stands alone and the flag is surrendered at its feet.

A STRANGE LAND

Billie Holiday's classic song "Strange Fruit" is a masterpiece, and I love how she talks about those old southern poplar trees and how they began producing strange fruit:

Black bodies swingin' in the Southern breeze
Strange fruit hangin' from the poplar trees.[8]

She's talking about the lynchings of Black bodies—across history, across this country. Lynching is a part of Black people's story: these lynchings and the strange fruit the trees would bear. Public murders and executions were attended by families and communities; parents and children would oftentimes come out to watch Black bodies be beaten, burned, and finally hung from trees. Billie captures this in her beautiful, melodious voice, singing about this twisted, excruciating picture of history. What's so funny is that then, people gathered to watch and see, and now people turn from these stories of strange fruit. The strange fruit is not something they want to hear about or see, but it's the truest picture of Americanity's history.

Americanity has left carnage in its wake. It has always produced this nationalism that makes those who follow it blind to anything but their political parties. But God reminds His children over and over again that this is not our home: This is a strange land that produces strange fruit, so we cannot put our expectations in the things or the people of this world. And here, "world" means the systems created that leave God out. This world is run by a series of systems that insist on leaving God out and glorifying that. Either you are running from God atheistically, or you are trying to become God—either way, God is being left out.

I often feel that the left is trying to create a world outside of the ruling reign of God and the right is trying to create a world where they *are* the ruling reign of God—but it doesn't work like that! We are not of this world. This is a strange land bearing strange fruit, and we have to learn how to live in this tension as Christians. How we respond to it all is everything—it's a big, important deal to God. With this in mind, we have to remember that sometimes our Christian worldview will shape the world and be in power, and other times it will be ostracized and persecuted. But how we respond to both scenarios is what matters to God. How do we respond when our biblical views and perspectives land in legislation, and how do we respond when they land in persecution?

This makes me think of one of the most popular yet controversial verses in the Bible: Jeremiah 29:11. Now, it's really interesting: Jeremiah 29:11 is one of the hardest parts of Scripture to read in context, but one of the most popular out of context. It's when the great prophet Jeremiah relays God's message to the children of Israel:

> "For I know the plans I have for you," declares the LORD, "plans to prosper you and not to harm you, plans to give you hope and a future."

This is a verse many of us find assurance in. We find comfort in knowing that God has a plan for us, and we trust it and use it to hold on to the hope that inspires, encourages, and empowers us. But what so many of us miss is the context: The children of Israel were in captivity. They were in Babylon—in a strange land that bore strange fruit that was in opposition to everything they believed, all their values, their ideals, and their God. The government and the whole system of Babylon were antithetical to who the Israelites were. Their beliefs were not popular, and so they were persecuted in this foreign land.

Believer to believer, what do you do when your biblical vision for how God wants the world to experience His love is not just unpopular, but under persecution? How do we respond to that? I think the temptation is to pray for escape: Get me out of this evil-stricken world! Get me out of this demonic place! Get me away from these legislators, this government, these schools and teachers and authority figures who are in opposition to what I believe is God's plan!

But in verse 28, Jeremiah shows us that God has a different answer for us: Stay. Marry, have children, build houses, settle in.

> He has sent this message to us in Babylon: It will be a long time. Therefore, build houses and settle down; plant gardens and eat what they produce.

What do we do when we're living in a strange land? With God, the question quickly becomes, How can we sing our values in this land that opposes us? He says that this is not the moment to escape, but to engage—engage with love, with values lived within your communities even when you're oppressed, even when you're persecuted. Don't escape or run away from this hard place. Instead, engage.

The other day I was at a birthday pool party. One of our church members was there and was eager to talk to me. He saw me, made his way over, and said, "Pastor, Pastor, can you believe this world? It's just crazy out here and I can't believe what's happening! The liberal agenda is making us become such a godless nation! My family and I are praying that Jesus would come back and, in the meantime, we're leaving California and moving down south. Governor Newsom is just going too far and doing too much. We already know we're going to heaven, so we've just been praying that God would go ahead and take us now. Can you believe the state of this world?"

Well, I smiled and nodded as he spoke, but I also thought to myself that escaping this strange land and its strange fruit, trying to ignore the history and not wanting to talk about it, feeling the oppression of persecution—all of it reminds me of God and the children of Israel and His plan for them: to prosper them and not cause harm. I think God wants to do that right where we are now. He wants us to engage and not escape. He doesn't want us to create another version of His call so that we miss the reality around us.

Now is not the time to escape from these issues and conversations, but to engage. And yes, there are absolutely times and there will be times when Christianity is not just unpopular but persecuted. Even so, let's not run away and let's not become victims of the politics of our days. Let's engage in the way that God has asked us to, so that He may prosper us. I believe we can have spiritual fruit in this land, and I think that's what God is calling us to: creating a new nature even while in a strange land.

A CHRISTIAN ~~NATION~~ NATURE

I think that in America, we have been so consumed with having a Christian nation that we've forgotten about having a true Christian nature. And honestly? That can be such a dangerous thing. When the goal is only a Christian nation, the goal becomes the nation, not God. See, this is in direct opposition to the gospel because the goal of God's word is not to create an exclusively Christian nation, but that the reader might be so impacted by God's word that a new Christian nature will be born from within.

When the goal becomes the nation, it weaponizes Christianity for our least-sanctified parts. What I mean is that when the goal is a Christian nation, we begin using Christianity to not just condone but to back up the worst parts of ourselves. Christianity suddenly becomes the weapon with which we shape the nation into something it is not and never has been. How can I say this? Well, Scripture was used to perpetuate slavery. It was used to green-light racism and mark it not as the abomination that it is, but as God's actual will. If we want to have the values and virtues of God's words, they have to come from a people who have His nature—and the truth is that we do not. We don't have a Christian nature, and we aren't striving toward one like we should be. We seem to think that pursuing the right rules, regulations, legalities, and laws is to create a Christian nation, but each of those things has to flow from a new nature before they can influence a nation, not the other way around.

It is so easy to weaponize parts of Scripture to back up and preserve our least sanctified parts when we should be surrendering them. When believers are not spiritually mature, Scripture becomes a tool of oppression, greed, and self-righteousness that ultimately leads to the dehumanization of Black bodies and bodies of color the world over. But the heart problem that has led to slavery and racism has not been surrendered to Jesus. Instead, it has been justified and sanitized so that we might create a new nation, and totally neglect the nature God intends for us to have. This is the driving force behind the abusive behavior by so-called Christians in American history: So many times, we have seen the word used to justify the worst of our flesh, and it is a sign of the utmost disrespect to Our Father.

Jesus didn't come to change a nation. He came to change our nature. Through that, He intends us to become a nation of nature-changed people pursuing not the well-being of this world, but the "well done" of God's kingdom. We are meant to be living lives of grace and justice with courage as we move past the power that has defined American politics.

I think there is an opportunity for us to become less focused on preserving a "Christian nation" and more expectant of God to move and create within us a true Christian nature.

You see, we live in this constant tension of "already but not yet": God has already overcome the world and we have the victory of the cross, but it's not fully manifested yet. These new nature people, who we call of the followers of Jesus Christ, do the hard work of living this out at a blood-stained table inviting all to experience the love and hope of Christian community in real time. By working through the realness of life with the expectation of God's kingdom coming to earth as it is in heaven, we bring to this nation, to America, God's heaven through the power of the Holy Spirit. In other words, these new nature Christians are ambassadors representing the embassy of the kingdom of God as we live in this foreign and, yes, sometimes strange land.

In case you're not getting it, here's what I mean: One of the first times I went to South Africa, I started my trip feeling very out of place. It was definitely one of those "We aren't in Kansas anymore" moments, and I just felt how foreign this new place was to me and my American self. Well, in South Africa is an American embassy. Through it, I got a quick little crash course on what embassies are and how they work because I'd never experienced one before: So, the embassy of a country in another country is legitimately part of that country. In other words? The American embassy in South Africa is in fact American soil—so when you step into the embassy you are leaving Africa and stepping into America in Africa. Inside the American embassy, the laws, ways, means, concepts, ideas, and structure of America are all in play. So, for all intents and purposes, the American embassy in Africa is bringing forward the ways, vision, and wholeness of America in Africa.

Dr. Tony Evans, a prominent pastor and speaker, said that we are heavenly citizens here on earth, and as we operate on earth, we are like ambassadors of the kingdom of God. So, as we live on this foreign land, we represent "a heavenly kingdom come, thy will be done on earth as it is heaven," through ourselves as living embassies of Jesus Christ. We have to understand that we new nature believers are meant to usher in the nature, light, hope, and promise of the kingdom of God in a nation that oftentimes stands in opposition to this nature. Our commitment, then, is not to the nation, but to cultivating a true Christian nature here in America as it is in heaven. Our attempts to preserve a "Christian nation" have been proven to be driven by power, dominance, and self-preservation, marked by donkeys and elephants. But I think we need something greater: We need the power of the lamb.

HAKUNA MATATA

One of my dear friends is a justice worker and a former veteran, and he was running the organization Harambe in northwest Pasadena before he got an invitation to go to Princeton to work on his degree for a two-year study on racial reconciliation. Now, Harambe is an organization founded more than forty years ago by John Perkins to come alongside marginalized children and disrupt the school-to-prison pipeline. Through academic help, performing arts, and mentorships, Harambe has helped youth in this area, which was once ravaged by gang violence and death, make it to adulthood so that they might lead successful, full lives. Well, when my friend left for Princeton, I got the privilege of being the director of Harambe, and I can't explain how exciting it was to see my friend get invited to a top school. This was about two years ago and my friend Harlan has since finished his program and graduated. Recently we were talking, and I just had to ask him, "You've been away for two years studying racial reconciliation. In that time, we've seen a surge of the Black versus white divide and how this has perpetuated America's history of abuse and racism. Now that you're done, I've just gotta know: What have you learned?"

Well, Harlan took a deep breath and gave me an answer I wasn't quite expecting. "Man," he said, "I think there are many things going on and many things between us, but one of the biggest things I've come away and struggled with from my time of study is that we just see God so differently."

I asked him what he meant. "They see Him as a conqueror," Harlan said. "And we Black folks see Him as a liberator."

Friends, I have been reflecting on Harlan's words ever since. Looking over the political landscape of America and white evangelism, I can't help but notice that they are losing credibility as they insist that Christianity is moving from a place of power to one of persecution. It just goes against what we know of Christ, and I think it speaks to how much we've misunderstood about how Jesus chose to show up in the world. See, He could have chosen to show up with a political agenda—with dominance and control. He showed up with power and authority, yes, but that power and authority were instead shaped by love and sacrifice. Jesus could have easily come in and overthrown the Roman government. He could have become the king of Rome and set up Israel to be this superpower in the world, but He didn't do that. Jesus walked in power and for sure had authority, but the way He used it is so foreign to us and this country. He used His power for love and sacrifice so that He might influence the world to do the same. He had rights, but He didn't come in with His right to overthrow. Rather, He laid down His rights and sacrificed so that we, His children, might know His love and live lives marked with His glory and grace.

I think we are grabbing the wrong thing in the political landscape and in this cultural war of rights. We've got the answer right—it's Jesus and it always has been, but American Christianity is trying to force Him through a filter of dominance and control, and that's just not who He is! That's not Christ. He didn't come to be a conqueror. Harlan was right in saying that people of color, especially Black people, see Christ as a loving, sacrificial liberator who has come to set the captives free—not to conquer them with His freedom.

Jesus never said, "If anyone follow Me, let them dominate." He never said, "They will know you are Christians by your control and dominance." No, He said, "Pick up your cross." He said, "They will know you are Christians by your love." This is the type of discipleship that Fox News and MSNBC and CNN will never show you. This is the posture that won't be featured on the news, and we have to admit that we have allowed ourselves to be discipled by these outlets more than by the B-I-B-L-E. We are living in an age where we are shaped not by the prophets but by political pundits. And I can't say it enough: Americanity will never lead you to the cross and sacrifice. It will only ever lead you to your rights and your self-righteousness and your ability to demand your way through control and dominance.

Political parties have proven an unwillingness to die for anyone, so they are unworthy of our undying allegiance. Don't get it twisted: I'm not telling you to stay out of politics. Have a party and have a preference, but just don't place Jesus at the center of your political party. He has chosen His symbol and it is a lamb, not a donkey or an elephant. He cannot fit holistically under either agenda, and we cannot force Him to.

Jesus is both conqueror and liberator; He is both lion and lamb, courageous and strong, meek and humble. And He calls us to live in this tension by abiding in Him. That's why the Holy Spirit and the fruit of the Spirit are so important—we cannot succeed and be transformed if we are not abiding in Him.

So how do we do what the Bible asks us to do? How do we lay down our lives? How do we live out the cross? How do we love God and then love *all* people? How do we honor our enemies and turn them into neighbors? How do we stay rooted in a space of courage and humility? The answer is the same across the board: through the power of the Holy Spirit.

Gabriel Salguero is a close friend of mine who pastors in Orlando, California. He often points us to *The Lion King.* Now, I have always loved this movie. I grew up with it. One of my favorite parts of the film is when they break into the song "Hakuna Matata"—you know, it means "no worries for the rest of our days"; it's a problem-free philosophy—hakuna matata. I know it probably goes without saying, but stick with me anyway: In this part of the movie, you've got your lion Simba, your warthog Pumbaa, and your meerkat Timon living in community together. Gabriel often points at this and says, "How in the world does this work?" These animals have completely different natures, and they are wired completely differently. In fact, the lion is meant to kill and eat the other two, but here they are singing together and bonding in community. The lion is a ferocious animal, and the meerkat is timid and small—they have totally different natures that don't go together at all. But what happens in the movie (and yes, we know it's just a movie) is that for the sake of community, the lion becomes a vegetarian, and the meerkat becomes courageous. They each develop a new nature so that they might live together in harmonious community—in hakuna matata.

I guess what I'm trying to say is that this Lion King idea is that we would have the courage of a lion and the humility of a lamb. That the lion in us becomes a vegetarian so that the lamb can become courageous. We must take on new natures to form a new nation that is united under the cross-shaped sacrifice of Jesus Christ and brought to bear on the Star-Spangled Banner. We must be led by a savior who came not to uphold His rights, but to lay them down so that we all may be free from the oppression and abuse that sin brings.

Our greatest testimony to America is our love for God, our surrender to His will, and the sacrifice that surrender requires.

So, friends, may God bless America as a conqueror of evil and a liberator of the oppressed. May God bless America so that we may receive the invitation to repent through confession and the truth telling of our history. May He bless America with healing and restoration—and reparations. And may God bless America to see the limitations of the elephant and the donkey so that we may come to know the limitless power of the lamb.

....

CHAPTER 8

DEAR CHURCH

BIRTH OF A BURDEN

After getting my GED and spending a few years in the workforce, God put it on my heart to go back to school. So, I got into and started attending Wesley Bible College in Florence, Mississippi. My time at Wesley was blessed. I had many relationships there with people who are still in my life today, and I was shaped and formed emotionally and spiritually by my years of study. I can attest to the fact that God was getting me ready for ministry both spiritually and academically at Wesley, and it was just an amazing season of life. But this season also came with some unique challenges that opened my eyes in such a way that I've been changed ever since.

So, a little background on Wesley before we dive in: This was a majority-white school with a few international students sprinkled in. Each class had about ten to twelve people, so this college setting was pretty small and intimate. It goes without saying, too, that I was one of the only pieces of chocolate on campus.

In this particular class, one of our big assignments was to go back to our home churches and critique what they did for evangelism: How did they evangelize? What were their main methods? How did they reach out to people? Once we did our research and collected our findings, we would come back and present them and talk about them before the class for our grade. Well, one of my classmates was this guy named Casey. A white guy, Casey went to a big Methodist church in Jackson, Mississippi, and their main method of evangelism was EE: Evangelism Explosion. If you've never heard of that before, let me give you a quick crash course: EE is a big movement where church members go door-to-door asking people if they know Jesus, if they're prepared for heaven, and if they've made peace with their eternity. Just right out the gate they're knocking on doors and hitting the people on the other side with some of the biggest, hardest, yet most necessary questions. I have to say I've heard enough testimonies to know that God really moves in this method, and so when Casey was presenting before the class, it was no surprise to hear how effective it was. It was all pretty simple: Casey would go door-to-door, talk about Jesus, ask the questions, get the people he was talking with to say a prayer, and then invite them to church.

Well, as I was sitting in class listening to this, Casey said something that would inevitably shape me and my ministry. He said, unprompted, "When we get to an African American's home, we give them the business card of the local Black pastor and then we go to the next house."

Y'all. I was sitting in the back of that class trying to process what I'd just heard: Casey's church didn't evangelize to the Black people they came across. Rather, they gave these people a card and essentially invited them to reach out to a Black pastor themselves. They didn't mention Jesus, and they certainly didn't invite Black people to church.

They gave them a card and moved on. So, I was sitting in the back of the class listening to this and I was irate. I could not believe that this practice was not only happening, but that it was openly celebrated by this church as if it were a good thing. As if it were a source of pride and confidence—like they were really doing something well. But to me? In my translation, all I heard was "We don't want you to come to our church, and we think you'll be more comfortable in a Black church."

To be honest, knowing what I know now, just thinking about what they would have inevitably encountered, I think it was probably better that these Black people were not invited to this white space. But the idea still stops me. I have to ask: Is this how we're building the church? Is this really how we're doing it? Is this really what we're happy with? Sending people to places we think they'll be comfortable and actively not sharing the gospel with people who don't look like us, live like us, or vote like us? Are churches built on some homogeneous principle? Well, I soon learned that, yes, this homogeneous principle was indeed in play because it's just easier to build a church with people who look like you, agree with you, and live like you. These people are easy to identify, put a circle around, and invite. This is the strategy to build your church.

But "your" is the keyword here. "Your" church, not God's.

Once Casey had finished his presentation, he waited for questions and comments. I didn't want to raise my hand. I didn't want to make a comment because I didn't want to be the angry Black guy bringing everything around to race. I didn't want to be seen in that way, but to be perfectly honest, what had just happened was so obviously problematic that I'm thinking surely someone else will say something. Heck, surely my professor would call it out and just light into Casey, read him the riot act, give him the business. Just let him have it. So, I stayed quiet, ready for the conversation to pop off and for someone to speak up. But the room was silent.

This silence is one of the first times I felt the burden. The silence of my classmates and professor grieved and deeply disappointed me. My feelings were hurt by that presentation and their subsequent silence. I really couldn't believe that no one else saw the problem. I couldn't believe that no one else saw the problem of what had become of their way of life, this idea that church was for people who looked alike and lived alike. This view perpetuated that silence in the classroom, and it created a chasm in my soul. I realized that the picture of the church in the Bible was not the picture I see here on earth, in this classroom, or in our communities and neighborhoods and churches across the country.

The church of Jesus Christ does not look like its picture in real life.

This brings me back to Revelations 7:9—a verse I often come to because it's where I get the picture of how the church should look and be:

> After this I looked, and there before me was a great multitude that
> no one could count, from every nation, tribe, people and language,
> standing before the throne and before the Lamb. They were wear-
> ing white robes and were holding palm branches in their hands.

This verse is where we transition away from the family table and instead surround the throne of the lamb declaring He is worthy throughout eternity—every tribe, tongue, nation, and race declaring, "Worthy is the lamb!"

This is our image. This is what we're going to look like. People from every race will be gathered around the throne. Can you imagine what they will look like? Feel like? Be like? It will be a big family reunion with Our Father, the King of Kings, the Lord of Lords! And we will sing hosanna forever and ever ... but that's not what was taught in my class.

I just feel that if we're going to be spending eternity together, we should start right now, and the church is where we practice. It is where we come together and execute this vision. We see multiethnicity and diversity all throughout the early church in the Acts of the Apostles and subsequent books. We see people coming together who have no business being together because they understand that we will be living out eternity together—and that's what the church should be now, not just then. We need to be preparing for eternity now.

But this wasn't being taught in my class, and in that silence following Casey's presentation, my burden was born. The silence has given birth to a burden for a vision that's clear in Scripture: Every tribe, nation, race, and tongue as much as your city or home allows. This is the picture of the church! But that day? That silence? I was saddled with the burden of seeing and knowing the church did not look like its picture.

WHATCHY'ALL DOING TOGETHER?

Shortly after I graduated from Wesley, LaRosa and I left Mississippi to move to Southern California. We settled in Pasadena, where I began working at the famous Lake Avenue Church. There I was one of two youth pastors; I was hired as the co–youth pastor because Lake Avenue wanted to be intentional about diversity in their church. They saw that their community, which before had been predominantly white, had changed over the years and become much more diverse. So, they wanted to meet this new reality, not run from it, and part of that was getting their leadership to reflect the community.

So, in I came, a young guy whose work had been primarily in the Black church. I was at a multiethnic church now, on staff with people who were so different from me for the first time. Let me tell you—I was having a ball! I was in this new season of challenges and opportunities to really see God work out this vision of biblical diversity—of what heaven will be like—and I was on this great, diverse team. In fact, our team was so diverse that I'll never forget what happened one day over lunch.

My team and I were on a youth retreat, and we all went out to have some lunch. Everyone was seated around the table, and I cannot emphasize enough how diverse this team is. We had me, the Black guy from Mississippi. We had Jesse, who at the time was a musician and he looked it: He always wore these big, black shades, his hair was three different colors (black, blond, and burgundy to be exact) that he wore in a very Flock of Seagulls way, he had lip rings and other piercings, and he just looked cool. He looked famous but the best part about him was his amazing heart for Jesus. He became one of my greatest friends. Then we had CyBelle, who spoke with a tone that almost sounded like she was singing; she was always so happy, and though she wasn't actually a Valley girl, to my Mississippi ears, she was the closest thing to one I had ever heard. Then there was Josh, this Latino dude who was honestly just so cool. The best way to describe him was like a twenty-three-year-old George Lopez—he was fun and funny, and he had this swagger that just made you want to be around him. Then, there was Jeff, who looked like he was from deep in Wyoming and could chop wood all day while at the same time be a full linebacker because of his amazing build and strength. He had the quintessential "white guy in a plaid shirt" look. All of us together? Well, we were pretty diverse. We looked so different that I'll never forget when the waitress walked up to us, stopped, looked at our group, and exclaimed, "Whatchy'all doing together??"

It was clearly one of those moments where you think you've just thought something you shouldn't say, only to learn a second later that you actually said it. But we all laughed with her. To be honest, her question was a testament and a receipt that we were beginning to accomplish the mission we had embarked on. Bringing people together who don't look like they should be together for a bigger purpose: Jesus Christ.

So, it felt really good to tell that waitress just what we were doing together: living out the gospel.

As I think about the church and how we should show up in the world, it should be in a way that forces the world to ask, "Whatchy'all doing together?" See, one of the biggest questions I'm often asked is "How do you build diversity in the church?" Many people and church leaders think it's a strategy of making the "minority hire" to create a diverse staff. They think it's putting the "minority" in a leadership position. Now, don't get me wrong: Those are good things to do and should be part of the long-term strategy of sustaining and maintaining a healthy, diverse church. But the main thing to building and maintaining a diverse church is being together with people who are diverse.

Diversity happens in community and in relationships before it happens in the church. Many church leaders want to see diversity show up on Sunday, but they don't do anything for it on Saturday. Saturday—the day you hang out with your friends, the day you do life together in backyards, put hot dogs on the grill, go out to sports games, play cards with friends, whatever. If diversity hasn't invaded those spaces, how can they show up in the Sunday space? Diversity happens in your living room before it happens in the sanctuary.

When we started Fellowship Church several years ago, community was how it grew. There was no big marketing strategy or email campaign. There was very little social media output. To be perfectly honest, we had no real strategy. We just opened up, trusted God, and hoped people would come. People did come, enjoyed themselves, came back, and then would tell their friends. That was how our church grew. But if you don't have a friend circle that reflects that eternal kingdom circle and you're not working toward building one? You will never experience kingdom diversity in your church.

I guess the big takeaway here is: Are you living in a way and building communities that has the world asking, "Whatchy'all doing together"? Are you living in such a way that the world will see you and your community and think, "How in the world are people so drastically different together? People on the left side of politics and on the right? Different nationalities and cultures and customs? What brings such different people together without them destroying each other, hurting each other, and instead makes them align on one mission?" Well, that's when we're able to offer our answer, which is the most transformative to the world: We're able to do this because of the gospel of Jesus Christ. Because of our love for Him and His love for us we're able to come together and allow something bigger than our politics, culture, and preferences to bind us. And this doesn't mean that we do away with our differences! No, this means we bring them, too, and offer them up as things to be celebrated—all of us together.

As we invite Jesus to make us one family, we have to remember that one of the greatest traits of this family is the breadth of diversity. That's what we're doing together. We're doing the mission of the one who loved us and called us.

CHEAP VS. DEEP

I have to say—I just love an up-and-coming neighborhood. When LaRosa and I were house-shopping and came to the community we would eventually purchase a home in, we felt excited about settling there—like, we hadn't found our place just yet, but we could see it. During the drive up to this neighborhood I remember seeing all these huge, empty, beautiful California lots, and I was just enamored with the possibilities and the choices ahead—just of what could be made there. While we were in this season of house hunting, I found a lot of joy in parking in new neighborhoods to see the model homes so I could imagine what my future home could be like. And, if you've ever gone and looked at new model homes, you know they have everything laid out: the floor plan, the rooms, the different types of flooring, the light fixtures, the furniture, the fire pit, the grill, the fruit in the kitchen, the bathrooms, the television—you name it. They stage everything you can ever imagine being in your new home and they're doing it on purpose.

Why?

Because they want you to see the vision they see. They want you to see yourself sleeping in that bedroom, cooking in that kitchen, lounging on that couch. The funny thing is, though, that the more time I spent looking around in these model homes, the more comfortable I got with them, and the more I could see behind the curtain. Here's what I mean by that:

The great flatscreen in the living room? Well, after a while I got up close to one of them to discover it wasn't real. It was cardboard made to look real using glossy digital prints and paint. The bedroom? Well, on one occasion when nobody was around, I decided to sit on that big soft bed just to try it out. I was surprised to find that that bed was as hard as a rock because there was actually no mattress—the whole thing was a wooden base unit with a cardboard mattress covered in layers of sheets, blankets, and comforters to give the illusion of softness. Honestly, the more I walked through these model homes, the more I learned that all I was seeing, all the great features I was attracted to—they weren't even real. At the end of the day, it was just cardboard boxes, paint, and some strategic lighting.

What I'm getting at is that my fear for the church is when they are trying to build diversity and spaces that reflect the kingdom vision, there's a real risk of doing nothing more than building a model home with the appearance of diversity, but none of the substance or follow-through. The closer you get, the more you realize that the values aren't real, and the ideals are just ideals. I fear that many churches want the appearance of diversity, but they haven't done the real work and, quite frankly, they don't want to.

With this in mind, we have to warn against the danger of cheap reconciliation instead of deep reconciliation. See, building a diverse community does not mean just making a couple of strategic hires so that you can start marketing your church as a "diverse" place with a "diverse" congregation. That's just making tokens out of people for marketing purposes. If that's all you do, people will show up, get into your model church, and then quickly realize that everything you offer is nothing more than an effort for cheap reconciliation. It's the old bait and switch: baited by the value of reconciliation but left afloat because there was never a true vision for reconciliation to follow and execute.

Value means something has a cost. It has a price you must pay, and so it is valuable. For many churches, there was a vision for diversity, but there was never any value behind it—so it ultimately cost you nothing. Sadly, I think most churches want cheap diversity that doesn't cost them anything and that creates a problem for their staff and church members who now find themselves trapped in a model home when they were looking for a church home.

Cheap reconciliation lacks value, so it can never reflect the vision of what you wanted because there is nothing behind it—and there never was. Cheap reconciliation leads to cheap decisions that make no real change, which leads to people leaving the church for a better option. In the last chapter we talked about the current great exodus of people of color from white evangelical churches. We find these stats of POC leaving white evangelical spaces growing because many of these churches opt for the cheap versus the deep when it comes to justice, diversity, and what God has called us to be. These churches don't want to go deep, and they likely never intended to. When racial crises came up on the news, these churches didn't talk about them. When injustices showed up across the country, they didn't want to talk about them.

I cannot tell you the number of times my phone rang during the season of George Floyd, Breonna Taylor, and Ahmaud Arbery. How, during that fraught season, Black leaders working at large white churches were so frustrated because they walked into what appeared to be the "model" church, and realized the TV was cardboard and the fruit wasn't real. The vision that the church had talked about was not real because it didn't have any real value—the bed is not one of comfort or safety that recognizes the pain and trauma that happens to POC in these moments of injustice and racially charged pain. In short: It's all a facade. It's just cardboard. Black leaders were being told what not to post, what not to say, and what not to do. They were barred from starting and having these hard conversations in staff meetings because the white church founders told them it's just "not what we do." So, now these Black leaders and hires were frustrated because they'd been baited and switched to work in this white institution that told them it had a vision for diversity, but that claim had no real value.

All of this forces me to ask myself these questions, and I invite you to ask them, too:

1. Do I stay working at this place? Am I fulfilling an assignment or am I being abused?
2. Is my workplace abusive to me because of my race? Am I answering a call and doing the work of God?
3. Have I just found myself in another abusive setting and relationship? And this time, not with America, but with my own church?

We have to understand that there's a great vision, and we have to resist the temptation to settle for the cheap. God has called us to pursue the deep, and it's going to require both vision and value—and that value is anchored in the gospel, anchored in what we believe.

CULTURAL QUOTIENT

Everyone's heard of IQ: one's intelligence quotient. It helps us measure our level of intelligence and quantify it, and it also gives us an idea of where and how to raise it. There's also EQ: one's emotional quotient. This shows how well you can understand and empathize with people so that you might develop, grow, evolve, mature, and show up in the world in a healthy way.

Now, I'm sure someone else has already thought of this, but I've never seen it included alongside IQ and EQ—CQ: your cultural quotient. This shows your ability to see and understand another's culture as well as how adept you are at learning about it, engaging with it, respecting it, and even immersing yourself in it. Do you know your CQ?

I think that if the church is striving to look like the picture God gave us, we have to have a certain CQ so that we might have competency and understanding of the cultures of the people we're trying to reach and share the gospel with. When we share the gospel, we are trying to help someone else experience something life changing. So, it only makes sense that we should know something about their life to begin with.

Honestly, it's like with missionaries. I have a friend named Rachel who's going to Papua New Guinea soon, and she has just two missions: to tell them the greatest story ever told, and to connect with the people on a deep personal level. The gospel hasn't yet made it to this part of Papua New Guinea, and the Bible hasn't been translated there. So, Rachel wants to go and tell them about Jesus. But before she can go, she has to spend years learning about these people: their language, their culture, their beliefs, their customs, their understanding of the world, their philosophy and way of life. She's not learning all of this so that she can "save" these people from cultural and societal norms, but so that she can come in with a level of IQ, EQ, and CQ that really helps her understand whom she's sharing the gospel with. The more she knows about them and their way of life, the easier it is for her to know the landscape of the life they live—if she's able to see their hardships and wounds, she can lament with them. If she's able to see some of their problems, she can bring help. If she's able to see their celebrations, she can be joyful with them. In other words, my friend is on a mission to love these people well and love them fully into the light and hope of what they were created for. But to love them well, she must first see and walk with them, hear their story, and understand their past. In such moments, we see God show up.

We have to have a strong cultural quotient, and not just for international missionaries but for anyone and everyone we want to share the gospel with. We need to understand who we evangelize to, the people and their culture, heritage, and experience. And by saying this, we all have to admit something real: Most of my siblings leading conservative Christian white evangelical churches sound like PhDs when it comes to theology, soteriology, eschatology, or homiletics. This makes sense because many of them are seminary trained. What I mean by that is they can pontificate and articulate and elaborate on these topics in such beautiful, powerful, compelling ways, and this is probably why they've been able to build such big churches—they know what they're talking about and can say it well. But on the topic of race and diversity? These PhDs suddenly become third graders right before our very eyes because they haven't developed their voice, their biblical understanding, or their cultural quotient on race and diversity issues.

Case in point: the Sunday following the murder of George Floyd. If you go back and look at the church services across America, you'll see that when we were in such racial tension, many of our white leaders were at a loss. I want to give them some grace here as I make this observation, not judgment, and as I draw some conclusions and—honestly—make some assumptions. I'm guessing many white leaders on that Sunday called their Black friends and brought them on stage that day to lead and steward conversations. Now, I want to be clear that I don't think there's anything inherently wrong with that. But to me? I feel it runs the very real risk of looking disingenuous because here we are yet again, and it feels like we're reacting to a crisis in the news rather than responding to the gospel and its call to racial reconciliation.

You see, I fear that many of my white siblings didn't feel confident on the issue, and so they needed backup and proof of their image of diversity. If that single moment was not stewarded well, it could easily have become a moment of cheap reconciliation, not deep reconciliation. If the only moment you had at your church was in reaction to the crisis on the news and not in response to Christ and His love for us, there's something wrong. If the only time you talk about race is when Fox News and CNN are talking about it, when there's a flash point in the culture and there's a protest or riot in the streets, then I'm sorry, but I fear you are only developing cheap reconciliation. Your cultural quotient needs to be lifted because we don't need to sound like third graders when talking about race. What that talk is? What that talk really is at its core? It's just about loving people. It's about God's call for us to love one another.

This should be at the highest level of anyone who names the name of Jesus Christ and dares stand up on a platform with the Bible in hand to declare the truth. If nothing else, we should have a high CQ and be able to speak fluently about turning enemies into neighbors, about loving our neighbors, about loving everyone in the family of God whom He died for. We must have a CQ to meet *all* of them so that we may love them, see them, mourn with them, celebrate with them, and just be with them. This should be our sweet spot, but for some of our white siblings, it's not. For many of our white siblings, this is their sour spot, and it shows. We have to make a change to make a difference that brings about transformation in the world concerning race and reconciliation. As it is, we haven't all done the work and it shows. Many haven't sat down and been a student, and it shows.

One of the reasons we saw so many apologies in 2020 during the season of racial unrest is because many white leaders have fallen victim to what we call IRS: Internalized Racial Superiority. Earlier in this book I talked about whiteness and IRO: Internalized Racial Oppression—it's this idea that because of whiteness, the sin of whiteness, and whiteness being held as the standard, people of color internalize the myth that they are less than in every way possible: less beautiful, less intelligent, less capable, less deserving, less worthy, and so on. It's saying, "Inside I internalize that I am less than and not equal and there's a level of oppression I experience and feel because I'm a 'minority' and because when I look around, all I see is whiteness. And if I'm not that, I am other."

What's so frustrating and heartbreaking about whiteness is that it flies in the face of that fact that God created us all to bear His image— the Imago Dei we keep talking about. He created us all beautiful, all loving, all His, all one, all equal—but whiteness comes and says none of that is true. And so IRO is born, and it shows up in big ways and in not-so-big ways. For example: Remember when we talked about theology versus Black theology? What does that suggest? To me, it screams that theology is white and normal, and Black theology is Black and other. Whiteness creates these divisions everywhere, in most all aspects of life: You are white and normal, or you are other.

So, with all this in mind, Internalized Racial Superiority is what many whites will feel and experience—and not maliciously or intentionally. I want to be clear that whiteness holds both white people and people of color in captivity, and so while IRO says one is less than, IRS says that "I'm white and what I experience as white is normalized everywhere. I don't have to go to a special ethnic studies class because the main syllabus is catered and designed by me, for me, and executed through me and my experience is normalized, so I expect to know more and be more comfortable in spaces that are designed for whites, by whites, and executed through whites."

We see it everywhere: higher education, the judicial system, the workforce, health care, and so many other systems that are marked with whiteness so that it is normalized. A white person can move through these spaces with ease and confidence because they were created for them: made for you, by you, and through you. So, in many ways, IRS allows white people to present themselves as the answer, as a savior, as the resolve, because the access and privilege they possess just makes it that way. It's just what it does—it just puts them there on that pedestal and automatically positions whites in most rooms to be the most educated, experienced, wealthy, and authoritative. They are on top and seen as superior to most, if not all, because the culture and the system we are operating in, especially in this country, has mostly been set for whites, by whites.

Like IRO, it shows up in big and small ways. But mostly, it shows up in innocent ways that are hard to see because people of color are dealing with their own IRO and so assume that "whiteness as standard" is the normal as well. This can cause people of color to automatically see whites as smarter or wealthier or as having more experience as the standard—and this is all unhealthy. This is why our CQ must lift and why we can't settle for cheap reconciliations because there are some deep things going on that require the gospel to help us see them for what they are: problematic and oppressive.

As an example, a good friend of mine lives in Memphis, Tennessee. Now, he intentionally moved into a poor neighborhood there so that he and his family might be salt and light in that area. They are a Black couple with Black children, and they live in a primarily Black neighborhood. Well, one day he told me a story about how he was at home with the kids when these two white vans pulled up in their neighborhood. Out of the vans came a couple of white folks and they made their way to his home, knocked on his door, and waited. He answered the door, and these people told my friend that they were having an event at their church on the other side of town, and they wanted to know if they could take his children to it to have fun and hang out.

Well, my friend looked at these people and took a beat. "Wait a minute," he says. "You guys just got these white vans, come into this neighborhood, knock on doors, and ask people to give you their kids?"

I'm sure you can see where I'm going with this so let me just say it: Can you for even a second imagine if this Black man went to their neighborhood and did the exact same thing? White vans, knocking on strangers' doors, asking for their children? Well, the white woman at the door had never even thought about it. While my friend was telling me this story, an older white church leader who happened to be in the room chimed in and told us he did that exact kind of ministry when he was younger. It was absolutely normal to him. But can we just take a moment to sit in the truth that that could never go the other way?

This could not happen to Black people. There is no way Black people would even think to do anything like this. But IRS gives white people confidence to go into these neighborhoods unapologetically and pursue these children in a way that Blacks could never, ever do. Can you imagine the reaction? The outcry? The calls to the police over "suspicious persons"? Now, let me be clear that I'm not saying the white people's actions were wrong or right. I'm just asking, can you see it? Can you see the IRS?

There's an episode of the show *Black-ish* that might help us understand the power of privilege and the frustration of losing it. On the show the family gets to go to Disneyland, and they have a concierge with them. This means that they have someone to walk them around Disney and give them almost immediate access to nearly everything. Having a concierge is a step above even the FastPass because you have a Disney representative with you the whole day whose job it is to usher you to the front of every line so there's no waiting. Friends who have been to Disneyland, can you imagine that? No waiting! So, this family is strutting up to the front of lines all day, getting what they want when they want and just having a ball. Before the day is done, though, the concierge has to leave, and the family is left to experience the rest of the day without the privilege they once had. Now, they were standing in line like the regular people, and it was the most frustrating thing in the world for them. The loss of their concierge has changed the rhythm of the day, the very dynamic of the family trip. Everything is slower and more complicated, and now they have to share time, space, and resources with other park goers who just weren't a problem before. They've essentially been slowed down and hindered, and it is very frustrating.

To my white siblings, I understand the frustration. It is frustrating to consistently feel like you're being attacked and having to defend yourself because this conversation of whiteness may make you feel guilty and ashamed. You have to suddenly move slower to understand other people without the same privilege as you, and it's hard when whiteness and privilege are no longer the concierge, but Jesus Christ is and He's ushering you to stand in line with others and experience the otherness that is normal to them.

My white siblings and friends, I encourage you to resist the IRS. Look into your social Rolodex and ask yourself: Do you have mentors of color? Where are you intentionally positioning yourself to be the student and not the teacher? Where have you intentionally and strategically decided to have someone speak into your life concerning not just racial issues, but all other issues that, with privilege, you just don't have to deal with? Can you submit to people of color in leadership? Can you trust and champion their intelligence and experience? Are your number one consultants on issues on race people who aren't on your payroll? Because I can't tell you how problematic that dynamic is! If you think you're culturally doing a good job because the people on your payroll have not said hard things to you about racial issues, then I think you're missing an opportunity to significantly strengthen your cultural quotient. Instead, you should go to events, conferences, and spaces where you are the minority so that you might learn from that experience and see your siblings of color and what they experience in this country more clearly. If we want the church to succeed in loving all people well, we have to strengthen our cultural quotient.

It's funny because I think cultural quotient can go a number of ways. I'm convinced that a strong cultural quotient in the church inevitably strengthens its Christ quotient as well.

So, let's call out the places where IRS exists. Let's resist the privilege and work through the frustration that comes with that loss. Invest in your cultural quotient because there is a lot to learn and a lot of opportunities in these lines—rather than at the front of them—to grow, to be better, and to be more like Christ. Let's raise our CQ.

LEADING COURAGEOUSLY

Leading courageously also tends to lead us to places of healing. Around 2009, there was a moment when I was now considered a kind of teaching pastor at Lake Avenue. It was a very prominent platform because whenever our senior pastor and my personal mentor, Dr. Greg Waybright, wasn't able to preach, I was next up on deck. And let me tell you—I loved it.

Well, around this time Dr. Waybright was preaching a series about God's unexpected family, and he was talking about the table and how there are people who we don't expect to be sitting alongside us. So, one Sunday Dr. Waybright was out of town, and I was up to preach a sermon in this series. The way I had been contextualizing the image of this message was the family table. It was just a constant picture I had, so I called up my California mom, a sweet woman named Robin, who just has the gift of hospitality in spades. She got everything together and set up a family table for me right there on the stage. Honestly, it was one of the most beautiful displays I'd ever seen: this great, long table adorned with this beautiful champagne-colored silk tablecloth that cascaded from the sides in layers. There were candelabras, the most beautiful flatware, and the finest china. The glasses on the table glistened in the light, and each place was set to perfection.

That Sunday, I came out on stage singing Bill Withers's iconic song "Grandma's Hands."[1]

Grandma's hands
Clapped in church on Sunday morning
Grandma's hands
Played a tambourine so well . . .

Friends, we went to church that morning. As I finished singing, I started talking about the family that sits at the table and all the dynamics that go with that. Now, remember, this was 2009, right after Obama was elected. The country was in a divided, challenging time. I remember taking that tension and applying it to the dynamics of the table: Republicans and Democrats at the table, the mixed reactions to the election results—the joy of some and the despair and anger of others; those who believe the undocumented should be captured by ICE and sent back to Mexico and those who were fighting to get them status through legislation like the DREAM act; those frustrated with health care and those losing loved ones due to the lack of health care and those saying health care is not a right and fighting against it, those advocating for health care for all—well, you get the point. I hit on every issue I could grab, and I did it all in a forty-five-minute sermon.

As I talked about how God calls us to love one another at the table that Sunday morning, in many ways this book began writing itself. This concept of the family table first came to life that day, and it gave me a vision of what the church should look like while not ignoring what can and often does happen when you have that much diversity at one table: Tension. Disagreements. Fights. We're all just not going to see things the same way, so how do we answer the call to something higher? How do we center this table and move past the politics and center on God's love and hope?

Well, I gave my sermon that Sunday. And around eight o'clock that night? It started.

My inbox began to fill with messages titled, "Today's Sermon," "Your Sermon," "What You Said Today." It was email after email after email of white brothers and sisters communicating some of the most heartbreaking, gut-wrenching, disrespectful comments I have ever received in all my years of ministry. There were some comments that said, "Your ministry has been a blessing to me, but I can't believe what you said today." Others said, "There is no way that a Democrat and a Christian could live in the same body." I had people taking me to task for even suggesting legal status for immigrant children, for daring to offer the idea that health care was something the church contributed to (side note: It's actually how hospitals began![2]). This idea was so foreign to the current reality of health care that to suggest Jesus ever had anything to do with it was just downright Marxist. People I had done life with, people I had pastored and shepherded for years at that point, said some of the most devastating things to me. Honestly, I still can't grab words to describe how that felt. I could only grab tears.

For the next twenty-four hours, my inbox was filling up. The church elders' inboxes were filling up. And Dr. Waybright, my dear senior pastor, mentor, and friend—his inbox was filling up. Everyone had an opinion about what I had said, the themes I'd presented, and the sermon I had preached.

By the time Dr. Waybright had made it back into town, he had seen all the emails and watched my sermon himself. That night he sent me a text and said, "I'd love to see you in my office tomorrow so we can discuss what happened this Sunday." And that's when it started. A fear dropped in my chest unlike any I had ever felt before because I knew what would happen next: Dr. Waybright was going to task me to give some kind of apology and take back my words.

Now, I know I am not without flaws. Back then I was younger, and I could have been a better communicator in so many ways. In hindsight, I see and know that I've always wanted to be a better communicator so, yes, I absolutely could have communicated that sermon better. But the heart and thesis of my sermon were biblically sound and biblically based. My message was appropriate because I know it reflected Revelation's biblical vision for the church and God's unexpected family. Was it the best idea to tackle all of those issues in a forty-five-minute sermon? Probably not. But the message and the content and the question of its biblical orthodoxy? There's no question I was well within the bounds of Scripture.

Well, after praying and with conviction from God, I knew I couldn't take my words back. But if I did, what would that do to my ministry and my ability to ever say hard or challenging things to our congregation again? That night, I remember sitting in our little California condo that was dropping in value quickly and significantly with LaRosa and our baby girls. We had moved all the way from Mississippi to fulfill this vision God gave me for a multiethnic church, for a robust multiethnic ministry. I was in the kitchen just crying out to God and asking Him, "What do You want me to do?" Friends, I have never been this hurt by a church family in my life, and I had never been so scared about what they were going to ask me to do. So, I pulled LaRosa and our oldest into the den of that condo and I prayed a prayer I'd heard uttered so many times by my elders back at Sweet Home. I could remember hearing my family—my aunt Vicky, my grandfather Eddie Jones, my mother playing the upright piano in Sweet Home's sanctuary, singing at the top of her lungs the passage found in the Book of Esther, "If I perish, let me perish, but I am going to see the king."[3]

That anointing from my old home came over me, and with tears in my eyes and a crackle in my voice, I looked up to heaven while holding my family and I said that prayer. In my mind, I was really say-ing, "Lord, I will pack up everything in this failing condo and I'll go back home before I sell out the gospel. I'll end it all and let this whole season perish before I recant and take back the truth of Jesus Christ and the gospel."

Emails were still pouring in. I soon had to make a new folder to hold them all. It's funny because throughout my ministry, I'd kept a file called "Encouragement" filled with all the emails I'd gotten from people thanking me for my messages and sermons over the years. After that Sunday, though, I had to make a "Discouragement" file folder. I say it's funny, but the truth is that all those emails, all that discouragement, caused me to question if I had ever really been loved at this church.

Well, the morning came and as I was driving to my meeting with Dr. Waybright, I had this overwhelming sense of calm and peace. I wasn't stressed or afraid, but I was cautious and a little uncertain about whatever was about to happen. But I wasn't afraid, and a peace beyond the outcome enveloped me. I was honestly preparing for the worst, but I invited God into that space with me and continued on my way.

One of the things I love about Dr. Waybright is his jovial, thunder-ous voice. He'd always greeted me with this really dramatic, drawn-out, "Helloooo, Brother Albert! So good to see you!" and that morning his greeting was no different. I told him it was so good to see him, too. Inside I took notice that our greetings were the same. I wondered if our time together would be the same. So, we sat down together in his office and had a practical conversation where we talked about the emails and the calls he had gotten. And then he told me, "Albert, I listened to the message, and honestly, everything you said I would have said." He took a beat. "I would have said it in a different way, maybe, but I would have said it." Now, I want to say first that I totally get and respect that, given Dr. Waybright's experience. I want to note that he never said he would have delivered my sermon "better," just differently.

Well, friends, in that moment I couldn't believe the level of respect and honor Dr. Waybright was extending me considering the gulf between us. His level of preaching, communication, and espousing of biblical, theological truths was that of a master. He was the former president of Trinity Evangelical Divinity School, and he is someone who has hired and supervised people who have done edits on the Bible itself. To say he's a scholar is an understatement. And to have him validate me and my exegesis? It was so very honoring.

Well, the meeting wrapped up well, we said we'd pray for each other, and I left. I knew that as senior pastor, Dr. Waybright had a big task ahead of him that I didn't: He still had to put out this fire. He was scheduled to preach the next Sunday, and though I felt affirmed and respected in our meeting, my new question was "How does this white leader speak to this congregation that has many who are very angry and have thrown so many accusations at me?"

Dr. Waybright didn't ask me to take back my words, but would *he* take back my words? Would he dial them back and minimize my voice and say, "Albert was just _____"? Sunday was coming, and I think I was more worried about attending church than I was about my meeting with Dr. Waybright. These people who were my brothers and sisters in Christ had been—it felt to me—beating me down. Of course, I want to offer some perspective: The whole church didn't feel this way. There were actually many who celebrated my message and gave me encouragement. But when you're experiencing that kind of trauma, you unfortunately don't hear the encouragement, especially not when discouragement is at its peak. It wasn't like I'd gotten thousands of emails either, but it was well over fifty, and that made it feel like hundreds. So, as I was heading into church that Sunday, I was afraid.

Normally, I would always sit in the very front row at church. I would be hosting the service at times, cheering on Dr. Waybright, worshipping, and experiencing the fullness of Sunday morning. In short, I would just often be a very visible participant in the Sunday experience. This Sunday, though, I went to the very back of the balcony where no one could see me. In that area, they don't even have pews you can actually sit in—they're all roped off—and this was where I stood with my friend and coworker Jeff. We were back there because I was thinking that if this went badly, I would be so embarrassed. People had said some horrible things to me, and I knew they didn't want to see me—and God knew I didn't want to see them. So, I was literally hiding at the top of the balcony, waiting to hear what Dr. Waybright was going to say.

As service got started, I looked down from the balcony and saw the family table from the week before. It was like it hadn't moved. Everything was there: the flatware, the china, the silk tablecloth, the candelabras. Robin must have been called back to set this up again because it was all there just as I'd had it the previous Sunday. And then it happened: Dr. Waybright came out onstage and approached the pulpit singing in his great, thunderous voice that Bill Withers classic: "Grandma's hands...clapped in church on Sunday morning..."

Immediately the church erupted in applause that continued as Dr. Waybright walked over to the table and began to reenact, step by step, what I had done the week before. He walked up and down the table, repeated my words, affirmed everything I had said and done last Sunday. I watched this white man bring honor and dignity to me in a way unlike anything I'd ever felt before. His words were healing. His courage was inspiring. I found myself with tears streaming down my face, totally in awe because I had never seen that kind of courage before, let alone on my behalf. And it wasn't that this was a superhuman feat—it was just that the silence had been so deafening for so long from white leaders that to see this man raise his voice in a melody of respect and affirmation for me . . . it moved me to tears.

That silence had been so deafening throughout my entire life, but what Dr. Waybright did and spoke in that moment brought healing to what my professor didn't speak that day in my Methods of Evangelism class. The silence after Casey had finished his presentation. It hurt me deeper than I realized. And now, many years later at the back of this balcony, I found healing.

So, when I talk about leading courageously, there's something that happens. Not only do we find our courage as we pursue one another in love, but we also find healing. When you're hurt by people in the church it's pretty devastating. To be consistently disappointed in a place where you should find hope and instead experience heartbreak at the hands of friends and Christian siblings is a deep pain. To hear "Your ministry blessed me until all of you showed up," even if that's not exactly how they said it. When I talk about race and my experience and my burden as a Black man navigating these spaces and how traumatizing and impactful the sin of whiteness is, and my siblings say, "You are no longer a blessing to me," it just hurts. It's kind of like when they told LeBron to "just play basketball." It's like they were saying to me, "Just preach the gospel."

But that's why I'm writing this now. Because this is the gospel

and how we came to this watered-down version of biblical restoration should break our hearts. The injustice, the racism, the malicious acts—even the acts that weren't malicious. We have to be held
accountable not just to our intent, but to the impact of what happened.
It's hard and devastating and challenging to sit in church spaces where
once there was so much love and now there is so much loss.

So, to my friends of color who have been hurt and disappointed by
the silence and the indifference, to those who've been made angry by
white siblings who haven't shown up much or at all in these issues of
race, for those who are navigating working in model home churches
that reflect the vision of diversity, but not the value: I see you. I see you
and I pray that God would bless you to love courageously, lead courageously, and in community by God's grace help our siblings to find
their courage so that we may all find healing.

CAN I GET A WITNESS?

The old preacher would be doing the hard work of speaking these
biblical truths to lift up the congregation and move them to a place of
repentance and renewal and even revival; the preacher would be working the passage tirelessly and laboriously to bring his message out, and
often he'd look out into the audience to see people looking bored or
disengaged. Glassy eyes, heads nodding, people falling asleep, even.
The old preacher, while building his case and trying to move his audience and bring levity to the room, in a moment of desperation and
hope for some kind of engagement, would ask the question, "Can I get
a witness?"

It's the equivalent of saying, "Is anybody out there? Did anyone
hear what I said? Can I get a testimony? Can someone sign off on this

idea I'm trying to communicate? Can I get someone to affirm and say yes, I have seen and heard and felt that? Can I get a witness?"

I guess the main message I have for the church is just this: Can I get a witness?

The church is called to be the household of faith filled with folks who have no business being together. It's meant to be the space where leaders courageously tear down walls that divide us. The world is being torn to pieces over the very things the Scriptures walk us through: racial divide, political agendas, kingdoms rising against kingdoms, political unrest, and corruption. It is dark out there and the world needs a light; the world needs a witness. So how do we live this out? How do we go above our proclivities and preferences and not walk in such divisiveness? What brings us together? The world needs a witness and we've got to see it. That's what the church is called to be: the witness.

It's this picture of and vision of what Jesus is culminating—every nation, tongue, and race around the throne shouting down the corridor of time: "Can I get a witness? In the church? In the earth? In America? Can I get a witness of the work I'm doing for the kingdom?" We are desperate now with the burden and the vision and the sobering gut check of how hard it is to do it—but we have to do it.

I remember when Dr. Waybright blessed me, told me he believed in me, and said, "You're ready." I had shared with him that I felt so led to plant a church that reflects the stuff that had been stirring in my soul for years: a church that from day one is designed to be gospel-centered, multiethnic, intergenerational, and intentional about making disciples and the outworkings of the gospel. A church that in its founding recognizes that racial reconciliation is the outwork of the gospel. That reconciliation is the call of the gospel. God is desiring to reconcile all things: back to the garden, to the trinity, the three-in-one where we dwell together in oneness and unity. God wants to reconcile it all and bring us together as one.

I firmly believe that one of the areas where the church is most deficient is race and culture. So, in our intention to build a gospel-centered church, we wanted to bring that to the forefront and double down where most churches have an unattended blind spot. In doing so, we created the Center for Racial Reconciliation to disciple our church in these issues and concerns. We created a space where we can unapologetically pursue the conversation, the issues around it, and the biblical understanding of it because we've seen what happens when we don't talk about it, when we leave it on the back burner.

This is why I see the current agenda to not talk about race as very dangerous. We will repeat the mistakes of the past if we do not acknowledge and heal from them. It's like when you go to college and have your core curriculum. The core stuff is part of your main journey in academics. There's no way an engineer can become an engineer without having taken stats and other math classes. There's no way a doctor can become a doctor without taking biology. These are the core classes you need to get ahead. But along with these come the extracurriculars—the electives. The classes that don't fit into the core but are offered as a special interest. Important, but not mandatory.

Oftentimes the church treats racial reconciliation as an elective, but at Fellowship Church we say no to that. It's part of the core of the gospel, so it's part of the core of our church. And don't get it twisted—this is not to put our racial identity above our gospel identity. But to do anything less than acknowledge it is to not see it, celebrate it, or surrender it. So, Fellowship Church has been very intentional about creating opportunities for racial reconciliation to be discipled into us as an expression of spiritual maturity and deeper love. We've created a space where we cannot live only in reaction to what happens on the news concerning race. No, instead we live in daily response to the gospel and what the good news says about race. We put in the hard prework so that when race issues happen, we don't stop and look at them, unsure of what to do or say. We know how to act and how to handle them because they are always and intentionally laced into our work.

At the Center for Racial Reconciliation, things are spearheaded by our director, John Williams. He was formally trained as a lawyer, and he contains such a God-given set of skills that he is a teacher, lawyer, historian, and great shepherd of people all in one. He creates safe places to have very hard conversations about history in America—about race, privilege, trauma, and the hope that we can have these conversations but also do life together where we reflect the value of the kingdom of God.

One of the cool ways we create spaces is through our Table Talks. Table Talks are themed tables that people can come to where groups have these conversations together. It's kind of like a book club, but not exclusively for books. What's more, we're intentional about who takes part in these talks. For example, we have a Table Talk on studies of white privilege, but it's only for white men. We asked, "What happens when you have all white men in a room, and they have a conversation about race privilege?" And then we created that space.

Honestly, what God does in these talks just takes my breath away. For example, one night in the group on privilege for white men, they were talking about privilege and what it means and looks like, and one of the guys got frustrated. He said to the group, "I don't believe in all this race stuff; I don't think it's real and this white privilege stuff is about guilt and designed to make us feel bad. I just don't buy it or believe it."

Well, Fellowship has worked hard to make these spaces safe so that people can express their truest thoughts and how they feel. So, his comments weren't disregarded or disrespected. They weren't agreed with, but there was a level of love in the room that was just downright beautiful. The other men in the group honored this and gave him space to feel how he felt. The next week they read the next chapter of their book, which just so happened to talk about the privileges whites enjoy in the conversation concerning race. Funnily enough, every privilege this guy had exercised at the last meeting, the author talked about. It went line by line: lack of engagement in the conversation, disregard of the issue even being real, and so on. It was almost as if there were a playbook on how to operate in white privilege, and this guy had executed it flawlessly.

You would not believe what happened in the following week's group. Before the meeting even properly started, the guy said to the group, "I want to repent. I'm so sorry for my comments last week. I honestly had no idea, and I am humbled to be a part of the journey. I have a lot to learn, and I am ready this week to be a student so I might come and learn and grow in this area."

I tell you, it was one of the most beautiful moments and one of the greatest testimonies. For those of us who do this work, I think that's about all you can ask for—not that everyone agrees, but that everyone approaches the table with love, respect, humility, and openness to learn from one another.

Another cool testimony comes from another group on racial trauma primarily for Black women. It talked about the trauma they've experienced due solely to race, and it was amazing to hear the stories that came from these women. So many of them spoke of the healing they received in places they didn't even know were wounded: wounds about their hair, their bodies—wounds from school and work and relationships. This was an opportunity to sit and acknowledge and identify and name places where trauma lived and then invite God to bring healing to them.

Friends, this is the work of the church, and this is the work God desires to do in us: bring healing to places that we don't know are wounded, and places where we didn't know the wounds ran so deep.

THE DRIVE-THROUGH

The pandemic was a very interesting time to be the pastor of a multi-ethnic church. I say interesting, but I really mean it was the hardest time. Everything felt so divided along so many lines: racial lines, masking, the reality of COVID, political upheaval—it was just a hard time to bring people to one table. It was a hard time to create a family environment when it felt like the family was constantly fighting on social media. Oftentimes I felt like a dad running into comment sections and telling members to go to their rooms and stop talking to their siblings like that. I was breaking up fights in comment sections and reading plenty of comments that just broke my heart as a pastor.

It was just a hard and, if I'm being honest, isolating time. I felt so alone, like no one could see me fully. Like I couldn't afford the risk of being fully seen as a Black man from Mississippi trying to lead a multiethnic church. Like I couldn't afford to let people see what I was feeling and fearing and the triggers I was experiencing, or the need I was feeling to have the same compassion and love I was pouring out be poured back into me. I was afraid about my need for permission to lament as a Black man without it being politicized, like it was outside of the boundaries of my pastoral role. It felt impossible for me to be honest about who I am, where I am, and how I'm feeling without having it offend someone or, worse, make them pack up and leave—which, by the way, happened anyway. People left Fellowship for things

I said that I never actually said. They left for views that weren't my own and disagreements I hadn't fueled. It was a hard time to be a pastor. It was a hard time for all of us.

But the pandemic forced us to get creative, and we came up with a Drive-Thru Communion event. After months and months of not seeing members and people not gathering together, we invited everyone to come and drive through this great big parking lot so that we might give them COVID-safe communion through their car windows.

Let me tell you, so many of our people were so excited. They even treated it like a parade—there was music going and people cheering and waving signs. But there was also trepidation about the day. See, we hadn't seen our members in months, and there was so much tension and worry inside about racial anxiety. As a pastor, I had been disappointed by the comments I'd seen from some of our people. Many were mean, unable to see their siblings or sit in humility. It was a mess on both sides, and everyone just seemed to be acting a fool and talking as if they'd lost their God-loving minds. The venom, the hatred, the back-and-forth, the inability or downright refusal to apologize—I carried it all as a pastor, but also as a person. And now here I was seeing people through their car windows for the first time, and as I saw them, I had no expectation at all for them to see me and my burden. And honestly? I was fine with that because the day was about them, and for that alone I was excited.

So, the line came around and I felt like I was the Rose Parade Queen: I was just waving at people as their cars went by, as they were honking and smiling with tears in their eyes. All these people were driving up to the Lord's table to partake and, oh, how freeing it was to do something that was even remotely familiar to what normal once was. People were moved. I was moved.

And then it happened: This car came by. Now, since everyone was wearing a mask, our best hope was just to wave and smile with our eyes. Well, this white lady who looked to be in her fifties or maybe sixties (again, hard to tell because of the masks!) drove up and she was waving and waving. But she stopped, and she was waving as if she wanted to tell me something, but I just couldn't hear her. She was at a safe distance away from me, so she finally pulled down her mask and said, "Pastor! Pastor!" but her words still aren't making sense to me. I must be looking confused because she then turned around and reached in her back seat and pulled out this cardboard sign. It said, "BLACK LIVES MATTER" and finally I got it. I knew what she was trying to say: "Pastor, I get it now. I didn't at first, but my daughter helped me, and I get it, Pastor. We love you and you matter!"

Well, it was unlike anything I had ever experienced before. At that moment, this woman saw me. And I wish I could tell myself that I didn't need to hear that I mattered, but I did. I so desperately did, and especially from my Fellowship family.

There was nothing more to say or do. We didn't have to talk about how she wasn't supporting the organization with her words, but only making the declaration. We didn't have to clarify, and I didn't have to ask her, "Do you mean the organization, or my life personally matters?" I didn't have to ask because when you love someone and it's in relationship, you know exactly what they mean. I knew what she meant, and she knew what I needed—and that's family.

Several other cars filled with families and life groups came by, and many had their own posters plastered to their windows declaring Black Lives Matter! And listen, I know this is a triggering phrase for so many, but in that moment? What we experienced was our church family coming ready to comfort us, we could hear them shouting our worth from their cars: "You Matter! You Matter!"

It was another redemptive moment I didn't know I needed, but I so needed it.

Fellowship, you've taught me what's possible when the church is centered on being the church. God has given enough of a vision, and I pray that we take on the value and understand this burden so that we may be the church we were always meant to be.

So, to Fellowship and all the other churches committed to this kingdom vision around the world, thank you for being a witness. And may we all keep begging the question: Can I get another witness?

CHAPTER 9

DEAR JESUS

A FATHER'S HEART

Several years ago, my family and I invested in a pool for our backyard. We had visions of grandeur for this beautiful, relaxing oasis in our backyard where the kids would play and get along together, and we'd just have fun for many years to come.

Well, as anyone with a pool in their backyard will eventually attest, it's fun at first, but after a while the pool gets rather boring and inactive. For me, though, our family is still in our active season, and when we're in the pool, it's an exciting time. It's the one place the kids will actually get along together and play well together, which is saying something since normally they're on their devices, separated in their own spaces, and doing their own thing. But the pool? When we gather together to just hang out in the water? That's our happy place. Now, I know the clock is set and our time is limited and that before long, the pool will become boring and be something the kids just don't want to do anymore. But for right now? It's our paradise and we just love it.

It isn't always a picture of tranquility and family togetherness, though.

My two middle children, Bethany and Isaac, at times have the hardest time getting along with one another. They often fight and disagree, and they just don't see eye to eye; if one says it's blue, the other says it's purple. It's just a regular tension that our family navigates, but I will never forget the day when we were all out in the pool and I heard screaming. I immediately looked over to see my two middle children literally punching, grabbing, and holding one another in the water—they were fighting. Not just fighting, but fist-fighting.

I will never forget that feeling of seeing them at each other's throats because I had never seen it before. We've seen fussing in our house. We've seen arguing and complaining, even tears. But to raise a hand at one another and to go toe-to-toe, pound for pound, in this all-out fight? It felt like a new level and a new low.

Now, I do get it. Kids fight all the time. Siblings fight all the time. But this was a new thing in our house, and I didn't like it one bit. I immediately demanded they get out of the pool and go sit on the side. They obeyed and sat there soaking wet, breathing heavily, glaring at each other, and then glaring at me on the verge of tears. Well, I went over there, and I became that dad: I lectured them for about ten minutes on how they are siblings, and you don't fight your siblings. I don't care what it is—you do not raise your hand and hit your sister. You do not raise your hand and hit your brother. You do not fight. You can argue and disagree, but you may not fight in this family. You are brother and sister, and it just isn't allowed.

After that, I banished them from the pool for the rest of the day and they had to go and think about what they'd done. As a father, I had to get myself together because I was shaken up. To be honest, I wasn't even angry—I was hurt. My heart was hurt, and my feelings were hurt to see what I'd just seen. To see my children whom I love dearly fighting one another hurt my heart.

Now, if this were a sermon and I were at church, I would say, "If you get it early, I won't have to preach as long." But since this is a book, let me just say, "If you get it early, you don't have to read as long." Translation: If I feel like that when my children fight, then, Jesus, I can only imagine how you feel when you see us fighting, hurting, and abusing one another.

When those of us who name the name of Jesus Christ as our savior insist on fighting one another on any issue, but specifically on race, when we insist on being so deeply divided that we lack the ability to hear one another and reach a place of racial reconciliation, it hurts Our Father. To see churches and communities divided in His name, to see His word weaponized to deepen the divide—

Father, we repent. We repent for not loving one another well and for fighting in a way that breaks your heart.

A father's heart always longs to see his children come together— and to be honest, a father's heart also longs not only to see his children come together, but to see his children come together toward him.

◦◦◦

One of the greatest compliments to me is when someone says my children look like me. Now, there was a season when this was not a great compliment to them—specifically my oldest daughter, Zoe. She's fifteen now, but when she was a little girl, one of the worst things you could say to her was that looked like me. Church people would come up to her all the time and say, "Girl! You look just like yo' daddy!" And she would look up to them with this confused, irritated look with a slight roll of the eye because, to her mind, she's thinking, "My daddy is a dude with a beard. Do I look like a dude with a beard?" But she just can't help it—she just looks like me. When she was born, she looked like me. When she had her first birthday, she looked even more like me. At two years old, she had to get glasses and SMH, OMG, she looked even more like me. It's almost as if every year that goes by, she just looks more and more like her father.

I'll say it again: If you get it early, you won't have to read as long.

Our Father's heart is that His children would daily, slowly but surely, look more and more like Him. That His children would look like their Father—that the genes and traits would be absolutely undeniable. The world should say, "You must be children of God because you look just like your Father."

Friends, this family theme really resonates with me for a lot of reasons, especially because I grew up in a huge family. I remember that some of our best times together as a family were at family reunions. These were when cousins from Detroit, Chicago, Ohio, Arkansas, and Memphis would come down to our homestead of Pearl, Mississippi, and we would just load in and have a time. It was easy to find us, too, because we all had T-shirts and it was a thing. Family reunion T-shirts were a huge industry when I was growing up. On our shirts, we would usually have the family tree and all of the elders' names on the front. On the back we would have the names of those elders who had passed on and were no longer with us.

The T-shirts were significant, but even without them, you just had to look at our family traits and you could tell we were kinfolk: You could see that Jones nose or the Garrison cheekbones or those Tate eyes—those traits were undeniable. At those reunions you'd see your grandmother and her sisters, and your great-aunts, and you'd see your mom and her first cousins, and you could see the resemblances and you'd just think, "Wow, we are marked by our DNA to have these similar traits and it is just undeniable."

Another thing to count on at the reunion was not just the T-shirts or the faces, but the feast. Oh, we would eat so good! We would feast for hours, and there were just waves of food: the best barbecue, sweet tea and Kool-Aid, and this big trough—not a cooler, but a trough—of ice and sodas. Oh, what a time as a young boy. I can just remember running for hours seeing those T-shirts and those family traits and feasting at the family table.

Friends, when we look at Revelation 7:9, it's kind of like God's family reunion—every nation, tribe, tongue, and race all looking like Our Father, all carrying the traits of Our Father: the kindness, the gentleness, the long suffering. Love has a name, and His name is Jesus, and we're all there looking like Him, like a family.

At God's great family reunion, we will be there with the traits of love and kindness and joy and peace. We won't have matching T-shirts, but the Bible tells us we will have white robes; we will be matched with our traits and our robes and yes, there will be a feast. We will be there throughout all eternity feasting at the family table. Notice: feasting, not fighting. Feasting and celebrating the oneness, the harmony, the beautiful love as we, as His beloved children, all gather around and sit at Our Father's eternal table of love.

Oh, what a great family reunion with our father, fulfilling the love of His heart.

SHOULDN'T WE START NOW?

Now, if this is our eternal destiny, if this is how we'll spend eternity, shouldn't we start practicing it now? Shouldn't we start coming together now, if only to know what to do once we get there? So, we won't be so offbeat? Looking like Our Father, loving like Our Father? Because that's how it will be forevermore. What does it mean for us to begin to put those things into practice now with how we gather, how we live in community, how we neighbor, how we do church, how we pursue justice, how we live? What does it mean for us to look and love like Our Father? Because the clock starts now.

His love leads with empathy and is marked with sacrifice. It is compelled to pursue justice and be drenched in grace. Let's look like that, live like that, and love like that. Let's look like Our Father, live like Our Father, and love like Our Father, starting now.

LEAD WITH EMPATHY

Therefore, since we have a great high priest who has ascended into heaven, Jesus the Son of God, let us hold firmly to the faith we profess. For we do not have a high priest who is unable to empathize with our weaknesses, but we have one who has been tempted in every way, just as we are—yet he did not sin. Let us then approach God's throne of grace with confidence, so that we may receive mercy and find grace to help us in our time of need.

—Hebrews 4:14–16

In Hebrews 4, the author goes out of his way to let the reader know that we don't have a God who's distant, far off, can't see or understand us, and who can't connect with us. He lets us know that He has been tempted in every way, and yet did not sin. He calls Jesus a "high priest," but you don't have a high priest who is above you—you have one who has been tempted like you, struggled like you, and faced the challenges you face. In other words, He understands. The author makes these things clear because he wants us to know that Jesus knows what it feels like to be where we are. He knows that our God, our high priest, knows what it's like to go through everything you will ever go through in this life. There is nothing we will go through that God can't—here it is now—empathize with.

He knows what it's like to be human because He intentionally put on flesh and came and dwelt among us so that He would know first-hand what it is to be where we are. We have a God whose love leads with empathy. He didn't want to just know us—He wanted us to know that He knows what it feels like to be in our seat, to stand in our shoes, to navigate these storms of life. He knows because He showed up. And that's just it: A big part of empathy is showing up because presence really matters.

Jesus left His home and glory, put on flesh, and showed up so that He might love us. In His love for us, He led with empathy and leaned into His ability to sit where we are and be with us. I can't say it enough: He showed up for us!

∽❧∾

Empathy doesn't require that we have the exact same experiences as the person sharing their story with us . . . Empathy is connecting with the emotion that someone is experiencing, not the event or the circumstance.

—Brené Brown

Back when I was finishing up my first year of college, something happened that really showed me how important it is to lead with empathy in every space. My best friends, Ricky and Jamie, and I were all doing life together, enjoying college and just having the time of our

215

lives. Ricky and James were roommates, and I was over at their dorm all the time just hanging out. Well, there was one night that I will never forget. We were all sitting together in the room, and we learned that Ricky's mom was losing her bout with cancer. There had been several scares previously when the family was called to the hospital because her doctors feared it was the end for her. But every time God would touch her and just give her more time.

This happened enough times that soon Jamie and I noticed something going on with Ricky. It appeared that he was living in a sense of denial, and we feared that if his mother actually passed away, he would be in shock and disbelief because he was refusing to believe what was going on or to prepare for it. Now, other members of his family were preparing themselves for the possibility of her loss. They were preparing their hearts and minds, but Ricky was living in denial—which, to be honest, both Jamie and I understood. So, we knew how important it was for us to be there for our friend.

That night we each told Ricky that we were there for him and we didn't want him to go through any of this alone. That night tears were shed, and the reality of her possible death grieved us all. At the very thought of losing his mother, he cried on each of our shoulders, and we just got to be there and be present with him and for him.

I remember praying a prayer that night that I still find a little odd at times. I said, "Lord, if you take her, would you bless me to be there." I really said, "Would you bless me to be there," which I know sounds strange because who wants to be there in the room when someone passes away? Who wants to be in the room for such a dark, devastating moment? Well, when you love your friend like I loved mine, you know that loving them well is loving them with empathy, and that meant being right in the room with him and loving him in what I could only imagine to be the darkest moment of his life.

Well, one Saturday morning Ricky and I were in his front yard washing our cars. Ricky was driving this beautiful red Camaro at the time, and I was driving my sister's Saturn. That morning we were out there taking care of our rides; growing up in the South during this time and season, you knew that washing your car was a whole thing. It was the whole first half of a perfect Saturday: wash in the morning, go cruising at night. So, we were washing our cars spotless, vacuuming them out, and the best part: applying Armor All to the tires and cleaning the rims.

I remember our windshield wipers were up as we began Windexing the glass and in the background, you heard the ultimate nineties jam by Tony! Toni! Toné!—"(Lay Your Head on My) Pillow."[1] So we had the music booming and we were jamming and just having a classic Mississippi Saturday—until we heard the screech from inside the house: "Ricky! Ricky! She stopped breathing!"

At that moment, everything stopped. Then, everything moved in slow motion.

Ricky was a fullback in high school and had a pretty fast forty-yard dash. I've seen him run many footballs, but I have never seen him run as fast as he ran from the car into the house to his mother's bedside. I followed him, walking slowly behind the family because I feared in my soul that this would be it. I will never forget the scene as I walked in: my best friend leaning over his mother's still body screaming and begging her, "Please don't leave, please don't leave."

This may sound odd to say but, honestly, one of the greatest joys of my life was that the Lord indeed blessed me to sit in that space with my friend that day. The next forty-eight to seventy-two hours were some of the most painful moments I know my friend had ever experienced in his life, and I just sat there. I got to be there loving him, empathizing with him. I got to show up and be present because, empathy? A big part of it is just showing up and being present.

Here's another example: One of the joys of growing up in Mississippi was college football. More specifically, SWAC Football: Southern Western Athletic Conference. Now this was mainly historically Black colleges and universities. In our hometown, the home school was Jackson State University, home of the Tigers and the Sonic Boom of the South Marching Band. Now, you have to understand that back then you didn't just go to the game to see the game—you came for halftime. People didn't get up and go to concessions during this halftime. No, everyone sat down to watch and participate with the band and the show they were putting on. If you wanted nachos or soda or anything else, you went and did that during the third and fourth quarters.

Now, what made the marching band so special was that the Jackson State Sonic Boom of the South was one of the best marching bands anywhere. They were talented! And our big rival was Alcorn State University, which was this college located more in the woods, whereas Jackson was more in the metropolitan area (if there was such a thing in somewhere as small as Jackson . . . but you get the point). We were the home team favorite, and Alcorn was our rival. Jackson was the blue and white, while Alcorn was the gold and purple. Jackson was home of the Tigers and Alcorn was the Braves, and I'm telling you we did not like them. It was about as good as a rivalry can get. As a young, young boy, I grew up going to the biggest game of the year every year with my family. We would sit right behind the band pit and watch them do their thing the whole time as we cheered on our team.

Well, I will never forget when my oldest sister, Diowanni, announced that she would be attending Alcorn State for college.

Friends, I was so surprised, and just couldn't understand why she would be going to our rival. Why not just go up the street to Jackson State rather than all the way to Alcorn? Well, I soon learned that my sister didn't want to be up the street—she wanted to be well up the way. So, she went off to start her college journey, and soon football season rolled back around. The big game was in November, and my sister was coming home for it. Growing up, my family would go to the game all together, and we always sat on the home side of the stadium, so I immediately saw a dilemma: We were a Jackson State family and my sister had gone away to school and become an Alcornite. Where were we going to sit?

Now, no one else in the family was likely thinking about this but me. Being a young kid invested in the rivalry, though? It was a huge problem. I loved my sister, but I also loved our team. I loved sitting behind the Sonic Boom, but this time I didn't know where we would sit.

Well, for the rest of the family it wasn't even a discussion, question, or issue. We got our tickets for the game, we walked right into the opposite side of the stadium, and we sat on the side of the opposing team. We sat on the side of my sister. Although Jackson State was our favorite team, part of us celebrating and loving one another well was our whole family sitting on her side.

You see, another part of empathy is not just showing up, but sitting on the opposite side. It's not enough to just show up in these moments. We also have to show up with their perspective in these moments. Empathy says, "I am not here for me; I am here for you. I am present not for my privilege or for my comfort, but I am here for you, and I am here to sit in the place of your perspective and not my own."

I remember sitting with Ricky that Saturday and telling him we should go to the movies and just get out of the house. But I had to realize that I wasn't there for myself, and although it was hard, and although I thought Ricky should get out and do something to take his mind off things, I was not there for what I thought he should be doing.

I was just there for him. My presence needed to be based on Ricky's perspective, not my own. I needed to show up on the opposite side. That's empathy. As the poet Walt Whitman said:

I do not ask the wounded person how he feels, I myself become the wounded person.

—"Song of Myself"

To my white siblings, this is something that is desperately needed in our relentless pursuit of racial reconciliation. The ability to lead with a love that empathizes and shows up on the opposite side, not the defending side. You cannot show up trying to fight off the falsehood of guilt and shame because that is not the goal of any of these conversations. No one is trying to make anyone feel guilty or ashamed. The point of these conversations is healing and deliverance. In order for that to happen well, you have got to love, and in order to love well, you have got to lead with empathy. You have to put on flesh and show up. You have to be present for your sibling's perspective, not your own.

You might be thinking, "Well, Albert, be fair—shouldn't we all do it?" The answer is yes. But what many white siblings need to understand is we have been forced to put on your flesh and understand the world from your perspective from the time we were born.

I once heard T. D. Jakes say on a livestream of a panel he was hosting at his church, "Whites can get a PhD and never have to learn Black culture. But a Black man can't even get a GED without having to learn white culture." And it is so true. We are forced to learn your world really early. We can't move forward without it. So, I encourage you, beloved brothers and sisters, to lean into our world—to lean in as Jesus did. To dwell among us, put on our perspective as much as you can and learn so that when the opportunity comes to love us, you may do so with empathy.

MARKED BY SACRIFICE

My wife does something that absolutely amuses me: She's a really great dresser, a total fashionista, and she loves a great outfit. But, friends, she doesn't just love any great outfit; she loves an outfit that looks exceptionally well put together and fashionable, but that she got at a great discount. I know she just loves it when we go to dinner parties or when we're heading home after church or when we're walking into a school function and someone inevitably says, "Oh my goodness! LaRosa, you look amazing! What a dress! It looks so beautiful!" I can just see the pride and joy in her face as she prepares to tell them, "Oh, girl! This thing was so cheap!" or "I got this at a discount! It was only five dollars at Target!" Oh, the joy she radiates! "Oh, these shoes? They were just two dollars from a thrift store!" She takes such great pride and joy in celebrating how good something looks while acknowledging how little it cost. She doesn't love the attention; she loves the discount!

Well, while that works well for things like my wife's wardrobe, it works terribly as a vision for how we love one another. Unfortunately, that very vision has become commonplace: We want a love that looks exceptional but that costs us very little. We want love on a discount. We want to see how well we can love one another and how little it costs us. I think we apply this to God, and if we do it to Him, of course we do it to each other.

Love at a discount is a fundamental threat to our ability to experience true racial reconciliation. For example, in 2 Samuel 24:24, David has made a mistake. He was caught counting his men before a time of war and there was a big penalty. You see, counting his men wasn't the problem; the issue was that he counted his men more than he counted on God.

As part of David's penance, God commanded him to build an altar on a threshing floor owned by Araunah the Jebusite. Araunah was happy to let King David have it for free, but David pushed back and insisted on paying them for the use of their floor. He said, "No, I insist on paying you for it. I will not sacrifice to the LORD my God burnt offerings that cost me nothing."

The idea here that I want to emphasize is that worship to God costs something. Love does not come at a discount—it costs us something. David warns us to be careful with offering up a love to God or to each other that costs us nothing. This kind of diverse, loving community that we're talking about—that God is calling us to—will cost us something. Friends, our lives must be marked by sacrifice as Jesus Christ gave His life so that you and I might have life. Jesus says to us, "Take up your cross and follow me—sacrifice in this manner; sacrifice as well." This love, community, and sacrifice will not be driven by our rights—it must be driven by Our Father's heart. And in order for us to experience it being driven by Our Father's heart, we have to first be received and embraced in a renewed mind.

In Romans 12:1–2, Paul helps us to see how we become a reasonable sacrifice unto the Lord:

> Therefore, I urge you, brothers and sisters, in view of God's mercy, to offer your bodies as a living sacrifice, holy and pleasing to God— this is your true and proper worship. Do not conform to the pattern of this world, but be transformed by the renewing of your mind. Then you will be able to test and approve what God's will is—his good, pleasing and perfect will.

He tells us here not to be conformed to the patterns of this world, but to be transformed by the renewing of our minds. In order for us to pursue Our Father's heart, we have to have a transformed heart, and a transformed heart comes only from a renewed mind.

In other words, love shouldn't be cheap. If you can love someone and you haven't made any adjustments, you haven't had to shift your capacity or make room, you haven't had to empathize, and it hasn't cost you anything, then I would argue the quality of the love itself. If you haven't had to renew your mind or change your mind in surrender to Christ Jesus—not in politics, but in Jesus—I worry you may be missing out on a renewed mind, a transformed heart, and a beloved community.

So, let this pursuit of racial reconciliation be led with empathy and marked by sacrifice, the kind of sacrifice that comes only from a renewed mind in Christ.

COMPELLED TO JUSTICE

When my sweet Bethany was just three or four years old, she did something I will never forget. We were out driving, and she was singing a lullaby to herself in her car seat—that old beloved song "Jesus Loves the Little Children"[2]:

Jesus loves the little children,
All the children of the world.
Red and yellow, Black and white
They are precious in His sight,
Jesus loves the little children of the world.

Now, at this time Bethany was also learning her colors at school, and while she was singing this song, it triggered what she was learning about her colors. You could tell that in her young mind, that song had triggered something that just gave her pause and she couldn't hide it. She sang, "...red and yellow, Black and white..." and then she went, "Whoops! They forgot purple!"

I know it's cute, but it shows us something deeper: She immediately acknowledged that if Jesus is going to love all the children of the world, that means He loves all the colors. According to her three- or four-year-old mind and her most recent understanding of the colors, it was clear that one color had been forgotten, and that was purple.

This idea of justice is not as simple as that, but it is as clear as that. We need a love that looks for purple. We need a love that asks the question "Who's missing from the table? Purple should be here; why isn't purple here?" We need a love that understands that it is an inequity and a problem that purple isn't here, so we must pursue justice to change that. It's an awareness, a conviction, to say, "It's not enough for me to be here, but purple needs to be here, too, and they aren't." We need to ask the questions "Where are they and why aren't they here? And is there anything we can do about that?" We have to ask who's missing from the table.

There's a powerful passage in the Book of Samuel. God says that Saul's reign is over, and He wants to anoint a new king who will be found among Jesse's household. Well, Jesse has seven sons but only six come out before Samuel. Samuel is holding the horn of oil over each boy's head, and he knows the oil will flow only when it's above the new king. So, they go through all the sons and the oil won't flow—so Samuel asks Jesse if he has any other sons because the Lord sent him, but the oil is not flowing, so something must be going on. Well, Jesse says that he does have another son, but it's just David, the shepherd keeping the sheep. In other words, David is insignificant. He doesn't matter.

What Samuel does next is worthy of note: Jesse has prepared a great feast for them all to eat and celebrate, but Samuel tells Jesse and his sons that they won't even sit down to eat until David is there. Well, the story goes that David arrives and the oil flows and God's work is done.

I guess what should be clear here is that as we are a part of this family, part of loving our siblings well is looking for those who are missing and refusing to sit until they arrive. It's demanding that they be at the table where we all have gathered. That means all marginalized people, whether they be people of color, differently abled people, those with mental illness and challenges, members of the LGTBQIA+ community—whoever they are, this table is as wide and as long as the love of God is, and there is room for everybody.

It's not about our tolerance. It goes beyond our doctrines and our theology, and the fact that our theologies don't agree doesn't disqualify us from our place at the table or discontinue our call to love. Let me say it again: Disagreement doesn't mean you don't have to love each other! It means you work harder to love each other more. God's justice demands that all of His children gather together and that each is provided a space and a seat for them to be seen, loved, known, and cared for. Agreement is not part of this requirement—we are there together despite where we disagree.

Jesus cares very deeply about His children seated at the table, and the cloth of this table is stained with His blood. It is stained with God's will and His love, and that's what draws us to and holds us at the table, not our agreement. We won't always be in agreement, but we can always have love. Jesus cares so deeply about His children having access to Him and not having others get in the way of that access that in the gospels He does something surprising but justified.

Jesus was heading to the temple, and He noticed that money

changers had set up tables in the courtyard of the Gentiles. Of course, Gentiles were not Jews—they were marginalized and on the outside. They did not have pure alignment like the Jews had, and the courtyard of the temple was their spot to gather. But in that spot money changers had gathered to sell sacrifices and they weren't dealing fairly with the people. So, they were occupying a space in a way that denied God's children access—and not only that, but they were taking advantage of these people.

In righteous anger, Jesus comes in and flips the tables over. He reminds them that this is supposed to be a house of prayer, but they've turned it into a "den of thieves."

So, this idea that love is this nonaggressive, noncombative force is just not true. Jesus' pure love drove Him to a righteous anger that flipped over tables as well as a system that was set up to deny access to God's children and take advantage of them. Jesus flipped the system over because His love is passionate, and it goes after justice. It pursues rights and calls out wrongs, and where there are walls, His love tears them down. "Love" isn't some passive word we can just throw around. It not only costs something, but it also pursues something. It pursues justice.

If Jesus flipped over tables, what does that mean for us? What tables of injustice should you be flipping over? Some of us are standing at tables, and we should refuse to sit down because others are not there. Others are sitting at tables that they should be flipping over. But I must warn you that it's hard to flip over tables of injustice when you're comfortably sitting at them. So, what does it mean when we see systemic injustice in our society and issues that have been perpetuated for decades? What does it mean to identify, name, and then flip those systems over? What does it mean to not participate in them, protest against them, and refuse to sit at them? Righteous anger is part of a godly love when it is focused on the right thing.

I want you to notice: Jesus didn't flip people over and He didn't flip people off—He just flipped the tables. Anger needs to be focused on the right thing because we wrestle not against flesh and blood, but against spiritual wickedness in high places. Let's call down the systems and lift the people up. As my friend Carlos Whittaker said, "Let's not stand on issues, let's walk with people, have hard conversations, and do the work of justice in the name of love."

So, who's missing? We must ask ourselves that question again and again. Are you willing to sacrifice and stand until they arrive? Are you sitting at tables that you should be flipping over? May our love be compelled to justice. And for our siblings who have been left out, marginalized, and forgotten, may we have a Jesus-table-flipping love.

DRENCHED IN GRACE GRACE

I've had the opportunity to go to Europe and while there, I traveled on their rail system. Now in that system, between the platform and the train, there is this little gap. Well, during my travels I saw it again and again: signs that read "Mind the Gap."

Now, I'm thinking, given that the gap can cause such injury, why don't they create a system that doesn't have the gap at all? Wouldn't that be easier? More practical? Well, the rail is already built. The train is already built. And the gap? It's there, and apparently, it's inevitable, so we have to mind it. We have to recognize that it's a real thing and it's not going to go anywhere. So how you mind the gap will make the difference between safe travel and serious injury.

With this conversation of racism and doing this work of racial reconciliation, the sobering reality is that there will always be a gap. We don't know why, but there will always be a gap and our humanity will show. There will always be someone who is offended, who doesn't understand, who refuses to concede a point, who continues to walk in a level of ignorance, who will say something that's just so stupid you can't believe they really said it, and who will fumble and try and still cause offense. There will be people who will do nothing at all and cause offense, and there will be people who will do something and then be accused of doing too much or not nearly enough. There will always be gaps and people who don't get it. There will always be gaps and people who do get it and just don't care. We cannot allow them to make us bitter or to cause us to give up on an assignment that they never gave us to begin with—an assignment given to us by God.

So, we've got to mind the gaps between our best intentions and the reality of our humanity. There are going to be some big gaps, and we have to mind them so that we may continue this work, this relentless pursuit of racial reconciliation, this practice that will shape and form our lives.

We mind the gaps. And then we do something else: We fill them with grace. And not just any old grace, but what I call double grace: the grace we receive from God. Can you imagine the gap between our works and His righteousness? Between our best efforts to love Him well and His holiness and goodness? The way He fills the gaps when I don't meet the mark—when I'm not who I'm supposed to be, when I try my best and I still feel like I'm not enough—the way He fills that gap is with grace and through grace. It was never about our works—it was always His grace. It was never about His righteousness and us measuring up to it—it was always about His grace and Him inviting us into it. So, where I'm standing is not about my righteousness or because I tried hard or stood long enough or did anything special. It's because of God's grace, and as we think about loving God, there's no way that we get to experience who God is without His grace. And friend, there's no way we love each other effectively in a way that brings us to the place of beloved community without God's grace—so you can't say "grace" just once; you have to say "grace" twice every time. It's a grace for us that we receive from God, and a grace for others that we might extend from God. It always has to be "grace grace."

So may our love for one another be led by empathy that shows up for one another. May it be marked by the kind of sacrifice that comes only from a renewed mind in Christ. And may our love pursue justice for all our family, and may it continually remain drenched in grace grace—enough to fill the gaps left by our humanity.

∽◎∼

I was having coffee with a friend of mine who's at a large, majority-white evangelical church, and he was just deeply frustrated. He and his wife are currently planning to move and leave the church simply because of the trauma and the abuse he's experienced as a Black pastor amid this white staff and congregation. In his frustration, disbelief, and trauma, he asked me the question: "Can this multiethnic thing, this racial reconciliation thing where we all come together… can it even work?" And then he looked at me with disbelief and said, "I really don't think it can."

Well, I looked over at him and asked, 'Does the blood of Jesus still work?" He looked back and said yeah, it still works. I asked, "Does His grace still work?" He looked back and said yeah, it still works. So, I asked, "If the grace of God still works and if the blood still works, then that means reconciliation still works. It has to."

It is from the abundant love of our Father that we pray this prayer: May we run in relentless pursuit of racial reconciliation and love for our siblings. Father, as we're seated at this bloodstained family table, may we never forget: How we love matters.

ACKNOWLEDGMENTS

To the lover of my soul, my Lord and Savior Jesus Christ: Thank you so much for saving me on January 23, 1994. My life has never been the same. Thank you, Lord, for this vision that you've given me and for the strength and the resources to bring this book forth. Thank you for reminding me, always, that how we love truly matters.

To my beautiful wife, LaRosa: Thank you not just for loving me, but for how you love me. Your love has changed everything about me and I'm so thankful to have found you in this life. You are the Lord's greatest gift to me and I wouldn't be the man, husband, father, and author I am without you. I love you. I'm so grateful to your family: your mother and father who raised you, your sisters Tacoma and LaTalla who have loved you, and our nieces and nephews Kennedy, Kia, Jalen, and Jace. I'm so grateful to be a part of your family and to be loved by you.

To my family—my sweet mother, Connie Tate, my father, Albert Sr., my sisters Diowanni and Larissa: Thank you. Because of you, I was raised in a humble home where the tea was always sweet and the love always flowed. I am the man I am today because my whole life I was seen, loved, and cared for by you. Your presence, your prayers, and your voice in my life have made everything possible for me, and I am who I am because of who you have always been.

To Pastor Brian Loritts, one of my very best friends, brothers, mentors, and pastors: Thank you for being the Jonathan to my David. Thank you for being the one to guide me, care for me, cover me, look after me, teach me, and ultimately prepare me for my life's calling of ministry. Thank you for all the preaching and teaching opportunities, for speaking life over me, for being a source of godly guidance in my life, and for showing me the way to each next step. Thank you for your friendship and for opening so many doors for me that I never even knew existed. There's no me without you.

To my friend and brother Ricky Jenkins: There hasn't been a sermon I've preached that you didn't walk me through. There hasn't been a trial when you weren't right there standing with me. Thank you for jumping off a cliff, Leo. "A friend loves at all times, and a brother is born for adversity."—Proverbs 17:17

To James Sutton: Thank you so much for coming to my house on January 23, 1994. The visit that you made had an eternal impact on my soul. Love you always, Bro.

To my mentor Dr. Bobby G. Cooper: You were one of the first to put me on stages all across the country. As we traveled with the Hinds Utica Choir, you entrusted me with leadership and I'll never forget it. You've changed my life.

Now, to the mentors, friends, and family members not mentioned here by name: Unfortunately, they've given me a word cap so I can't list each and every one of you on my heart. But the beautiful thing about our relationship is that you know exactly who you are and how much I love you. So thank you for being in relationship with me. Thank you for your kindness and investment in my life.

Finally, to Fellowship:

To the staff: I am overwhelmed every day I get to work with you. Over the years, you've made me so much better. Thank you so much for your leadership and your commitment to this vision.

To my Fellowship family: You've given me renewed hope in how I see the power of the church in the world. You've shown me the life and fierce love of the family of faith. Thank you for being the greatest faith community I could have ever dreamed of. Thank you for staying at the table.

NOTES

CHAPTER 1: DEAR READER
1 Korie Little Edwards. *The Elusive Dream: The Power of Race in Interracial Churches*. N.p.: Oxford University Press US, 2021 (originally published 2008).

CHAPTER 2: DEAR SIBLINGS
1 Matt. 22:36–40; Mark 12:28–31; Luke 10:27; John 13:34.
2 Eph. 3:1–6.
3 Paul Baloche. "Open the Eyes of My Heart." Track 4 on *Open the Eyes of My Heart*. Integrity Music, 2000, CD.
4 John 4.
5 *Coming to America*. Directed by John Landis. Hollywood: Paramount Pictures, 1988.

CHAPTER 3: DEAR MISSISSIPPI
1 "Medgar Evers." NAACP. https://www.naacp.org/naacp-history-medgar-evers/. Retrieved May 11, 2021.
2 Bessel A. Van der Kolk. *The Body Keeps the Score: Brain, Mind, and Body in the Healing of Trauma*. New York: Penguin Books, 2015.

3 Courtney L. McCluney et al. "The Cost of Code-Switching." *Harvard Business Review*, November 15, 2019. https://hbr.org/2019/11/the-costs -of-codeswitching.

4 Timothy B. Tyson. *The Blood of Emmett Till*. New York: Simon & Schuster, 2018.

5 Amir Vera and Laura Ly. "White Woman Who Called Police on a Black Man Bird-Watching in Central Park Has Been Fired." CNN, May 26, 2020. https://www.cnn.com/2020/05/26/us/central-park-video-dog-video -african-american-trnd/index.html.

6 Ben Wasserman. "Don Cheadle, *Golden Girls'* Blanche's Confederate Flag Scenes Resurface." CBR.com, July 2, 2020. https://www.cbr.com /don-cheadle-golden-girls-confederate-flag-scene/.

CHAPTER 4: DEAR WHITENESS

1 *Malcolm X*. Directed by Spike Lee. Burbank: Warner Bros., 1992.

CHAPTER 5: DEAR BEREAVED

1 Camille Caldera. "Fact Check: Rates of White-on-White and Black-on-Black Crime Are Similar." *USA Today*, September 29, 2020. https:// www.usatoday.com/story/news/factcheck/2020/09/29/fact-check-meme -shows-incorrect-homicide-stats-race/5739522002/.

CHAPTER 6: DEAR ANCESTORS

1 From The Spirituals Project of the University of Denver, "African Tradition, Proverbs, and Sankofa."

2 Barron H. Lerner. "Scholars Argue Over Legacy of Surgeon Who Was Lionized, Then Vilified." *New York Times*, October 28, 2003. https:// www.nytimes.com/2003/10/28/health/scholars-argue-over-legacy-of -surgeon-who-was-lionized-then-vilified.html. Archived from the original on February 22, 2015. Retrieved February 17, 2021.

3 Benjamin Butanis. "The Legacy of Henrietta Lacks." Johns Hopkins Medicine. March 9, 2020. https://www.hopkinsmedicine.org/henrietta lacks/.

4 Carlotta Gall. "In Turkey's Failed Coup, Trainees Face the Same Stiff Punishments as Generals." *New York Times*, April 3, 2021. https://www

.nytimes.com/2021/04/03/world/europe/turkey-coup-trainee-pilots .html. Accessed July 10, 2021.

CHAPTER 7: DEAR AMERICA

1 "Lynching in America: Confronting the Legacy of Racial Terror," 3rd ed. Equal Justice Initiative. https://lynchinginamerica.eji.org/report/. Accessed July 10, 2021.

2 Private Silas Bradshaw, to Lieutenant Graster, June 22, 1918. Smithsonian National Postal Museum. https://postalmuseum.si.edu/exhibition/my-fellow -soldiers-exhibition-explore-by-theme-mobilizing/private-silas-bradshaw-to.

3 Dr. Adam M. Robinson Jr. "Commentary: Nation's Black Military Veterans Deserve Better." *Montana Standard*, January 12, 2018. https://mt standard.com/commentary-nation-s-black-military-veterans-deserve-bet ter/article_6ab5fcb5-5545-595f-b656-0e37de31ec82.html.

4 Stephen Sawchuk. "What Is Critical Race Theory, and Why Is It Under Attack?" *Education Week*, May 18, 2021. https://www.edweek.org/lead ership/what-is-critical-race-theory-and-why-is-it-under-attack/2021/05.

5 Martin Luther King Jr. "Letter from a Birmingham Jail." April 1963. CSU, Chico, website. https://www.csuchico.edu/iege/_assets/documents /susi-letter-from-birmingham-jail.pdf. Accessed October 12, 2021.

6 *The Great Debaters*. Directed by Denzel Washington. West Hollywood: Harpo Productions, 2007.

7 "Microaggression." *Oxford Dictionary*. Lexico. https://www.lexico.com /en/definition/microaggression.

8 Billie Holiday. Written and composed by Abel Meeropol. "Strange Fruit." Published 1937. Recorded, Commodore. 1939, vinyl.

CHAPTER 8: DEAR CHURCH

1 Bill Withers. "Grandma's Hands." Track 3 on *Just as I Am*. Sussex Records, 1971, LP.

2 Edward Whelan. "Christianity and the Rise of the Hospital in the Ancient World." *Classical Wisdom Weekly*, March 27, 2020. https://classi calwisdom.com/culture/history/christianity-and-the-rise-of-the-hospi tal-in-the-ancient-world/. Accessed July 10, 2021.

3 Esther 4:16.

CHAPTER 9: DEAR JESUS

1 Tony! Toni! Toné! "(Lay Your Head on My) Pillow." Track 7 on *Sons of Soul*. Paradise Recording Studio. 1993, cassette.

2 The lyrics, written by Clare Herbert Woolston in the late 1800s, were set by composer George F. Root to the tune of "Tramp, Tramp, Tramp (We Go A-Marching)," which had been sung by foot soldiers in the Civil War.